TRANSFORMING DAILY WORK
INTO A DIVINE VOCATION

Transforming Daily Work into a Divine Vocation

∽

ROBERT BANKS

▲ CASCADE *Books* • Eugene, Oregon

TRANSFORMING DAILY WORK INTO A DIVINE VOCATION

Copyright © 2022 Robert Banks. All rights reserved. Except for brief quotations in critical publications or reviews, no part of this book may be reproduced in any manner without prior written permission from the publisher. Write: Permissions, Wipf and Stock Publishers, 199 W. 8th Ave., Suite 3, Eugene, OR 97401.

Cascade Books
An Imprint of Wipf and Stock Publishers
199 W. 8th Ave., Suite 3
Eugene, OR 97401

www.wipfandstock.com

PAPERBACK ISBN: 978-1-6667-3118-7
HARDCOVER ISBN: 978-1-6667-2339-7
EBOOK ISBN: 978-1-6667-2340-3

Cataloguing-in-Publication data:

Names: Banks, Robert.

Title: Transforming daily work into a divine vocation / Robert Banks.

Description: Eugene, OR: Cascade Books, 2022 | Includes bibliographical references.

Identifiers: ISBN 978-1-6667-3118-7 (paperback) | ISBN 978-1-6667-2339-7 (hardcover) | ISBN 978-1-6667-2340-3 (ebook)

Subjects: Work—Religious aspects—Christianity. Vocation—Christianity. Christian life.

Classification: BT738.5 B365 2022 (print) | BT7385 (ebook)

Table of Contents

Prologue: The Connection between Faith and the Workplace vii

PART 1: *Why Do We Engage in Work?*

1. Biblical Foundation: Work—From Genesis to Revelation 5
2. Theological Perspective: God—The First and Model Worker 14
3. Historical Development: Vocation—A Whole-Life View 22

PART 2: *What Difference Does Vocation Make?*

4. Some Exemplary Job Descriptions 35
5. A New-Settler Farmer: Cultivating and Resettling the Creation 40
6. A Bank Manager: Reflecting Christ in the Financial Industry 50
7. A Builder-Developer: Responsible Steward of God's Resources 59
8. A Business Owner: Christian Mission in a Car Sales Firm 68
9. A Cooperative Founder: Craftworker as Marketplace Apostle 77
10. A Research Economist: Seeking the Welfare of an Island Community 86
11. A Television Journalist: Glorifying God through Truth-Telling in Media 95

PART 3: *How Can We Be Faithful to Our Calling?*

12. Discerning Personal Vocation in Everyday Settings 107
13. Increasing Job Turnover and the Casualizing of Work 119
14. Maintaining Integrity and Valid Compromises 126

Epilogue: Does Our Work Have Any Eternal Value? 135
Resources 139
Bibliography 140

Prologue

I HAVE LONG HAD a interest in the connection between faith and the workplace. This began after a move from teaching biblical studies at Macquarie University in Sydney to working with lay people in Canberra on integrating their faith with their everyday lives. The challenge in doing this was first highlighted while organizing a series of campus-wide lectures in the Australian National University, at which a range of Christian academics were invited to talk about how they linked their religious convictions with their teaching and research. Disappointingly, only about one in four was able to do this in a way beyond seeing the two as complementary rather than interconnected. The few who presented a coherent vision, however, had a noticeable impact upon the very diverse audience.

Investigating this discrepancy further revealed how much the growing problem of busyness was a factor in the partial disconnect between faith and ordinary work. I addressed this issue in a book on *The Tyranny of Time,* which asked whether for many people work was tending to have an idolatrous place in modern societies. Alongside this, I was drawn into a three-year project with the Zadok Institute for Christianity and Society in Canberra, examining how senior Christian public servants viewed the relevance of their values to the way they advised and implemented government policy. This led to consultations of public servants in various parts of the country and finally a national conference whose proceedings were published in a book on *Private Values and Public Policy: The Ethics of Decision-Making in Government Administration,* which became a resource for training key prospective personnel. Shortly afterwards, I endeavored to address the lack of adequate theological treatment of work and other aspects of everyday activities in *All the Business of Life: Bringing Theology Down to Earth.*

Prologue

During an overseas sabbatical year in the mid-eighties, I was able to network with several others interested in faith-work integration. When I was offered a foundation professorship in the Ministry of the Laity at Fuller Theological Seminary in Los Angeles, other possibilities opened up. These included helping to develop a lay-initiated, cross-denominational *Ministry of Daily Life* network and annual conference focused on workplace issues; co-teaching a graduate course on values in the workplace that used students' own work experiences as case studies; and a book that contained some exemplary workplace profiles, *Faith Goes to Work: Reflections from the Marketplace*.

During this time, a number of well-established Christians in Hollywood approached the seminary about organizing regular informal meetings with them. They were looking for something along the lines of the Inklings group around C. S. Lewis to discuss the way their faith did and should inform their work as a director, producer, screenwriter, etc. We met monthly over the following decade, and developed an annual City of the Angels film festival that screened and discussed films from a spiritual perspective as well as an accompanying seminar that brought filmmakers and ministers together. When I was invited to head up the seminary's new De Pree Center for Leadership, the way opened up to develop a range of resources for Christians in business, the professions, and media, as well as contribute to annual conferences of such organizations as State Farm Insurance, Young Leaders of America, and World Vision International.

On returning to Australia, directing a Christian Studies Institute connected to a major university enabled the creation of undergraduate courses that connected theology and life and professional development seminars for several occupations on integrating work and faith. Out of this arose an international consultation on the subject that attracted participants from Asia, Europe, and North America. My wife Linda and I also collaborated on an eight-session Bible discussion guide entitled *Going to Work with God*. Along with teaching occasionally on this topic at the lay-oriented Biblical Graduate School of Theology in Singapore, an invitation came to write a monograph on *Daily Work as Divine Vocation* for an Asian audience. Back home in Australia, becoming a theological consultant to the public think tank ReVenture resulted in writing three Occasional Papers on significant changes occurring in the workplaces today.

I mention these various activities to show that this text springs from practical involvement as well as academic reflection. All these experiences

PROLOGUE

have contributed to the making of this book. With the generous permission of Dr. Roland Chia of the Centre for Public Christianity in Singapore, it includes a revised version of three chapters from *Daily Work as Divine Vocation,* which so far has only been available in Asia. It also incorporates six case studies from *Faith Goes to Work,* first published by the Alban Institute in Washington, and later reprinted by Wipf and Stock Publishers. Lindsay MacMillan, of ReVenture Australia, endorsed my drawing on two *Theological Responses* to current workplace issues they had invited me to write. In each of the three parts of the volume, some new material has also been added

My thanks are due to Michael Thomson for initially suggesting a book drawing on some of my previous writings, and to Rodney Clapp, who I have been delighted to connect with again on this rewarding enterprise.

Robert Banks

Canberra
July, 1, 2021

Part 1

Why Do We Engage in Work?

Introduction

WORK IS A BASIC feature of life. Most of it happens in workplaces of various kinds, but increasingly, only in part caused by the pandemic, also in homes. Work is classified into full-time and part-time, regular and casual, year-round or seasonal. For most of us, it occupies the main hours of our weekdays, but sometimes part of our evenings and weekends as well. It now occupies more of our hours than any other activity, including sleep. People are preoccupied with their work. The pressures they encounter there, the ethical dilemmas they face, the conflicts between job and family, and the threat of unemployment occupy a growing amount of their energy and time. For many, there is a greater reality and community in their place of work than in their family life or even their church.

While paid employment is the chief form of work, and the one chiefly in mind in this book, there is also voluntary work, housework, and school work or study. What follows is also applicable to these, especially where they are—at least for a time—the main form of a person's work.

Why do we work? We do so for one or more of the following reasons:

- to earn enough money to support ourselves and others who may be dependent on us;
- to do something useful or productive in some way in our wider community;

- to train or prepare for a kind of work that fits our interests, skills, and training; to make a genuine difference in the lives of others or to our world more generally;
- to fulfill a divine calling to the kind of work we feel we should pursue.

These are all valid reasons for working. Often, however, they are mixed up with other motives that are questionable:

- my work gives me a sense of identity that otherwise I would not possess;
- my work gives me money and status and therefore more significance than others;
- my work creates the opportunity to exercise power and control over colleagues.

These motives stem from a sense of insecurity, personal importance, or self-absorbed tendencies. In previous centuries, and for lower-paid workers today, earning enough money to support a family was a major preoccupation. Over the last few decades, more prominence has been given to finding work that fits our interests and abilities. Today, more people are looking for work that will make a difference to their society and fulfill their own deeper desires. This shift is well described in a recent report:

> Purpose and meaning are playing an increasingly important role in the contemporary workforce. In particular, the younger generations entering the workforce are looking for "meaning makers," people who can help them locate their work in the context of a bigger story and life purpose. At the same time writers and researchers across multiple disciplines are re-awakening to the place of not only purpose and meaning, but also emotions and spirituality in the workplace, and their importance for organizational effectiveness.[1]

While, in general, finding purpose and meaning in work rates more highly in Western rather than Asian societies, in these too many are now seeking greater involvement in what they do. These people are also concerned about values in the workplace—for example, respect, recognition, and care. Younger workers, however, look increasingly for personal growth, self-fulfillment, professional development, and a supportive environment.

---

1. Becket and MacMillan, *Purpose of Life*, 4, 7, 11.

Introduction to Part 1

Studies of Generation Y highlight an interest in empowerment and career growth, training and development, and work-life harmony. Nearly half of these indicate that, given the choice, they would like to leave their current employers in the next two years.[2] While more employers now acknowledge the importance of these concerns, most are still not responding effectively to them.

This situation is not helped by certain wider developments. Over the last century, traditional sources for discovering purpose, meaning, and values in life have lost influence. Fitting in with family expectations has decreased in importance, even in more traditional societies. Churches tend to focus increasingly on members' personal growth and family responsibilities. Where work does come into view, it is mostly in limited or inadequate ways:

- While, as in the helping professions, work may provide a context for serving God, it is not a form of ministry.
- God's main concern is that employees work hard, are obedient to employers, are honest in their dealings, and share their faith.
- A prime reason for work is to financially support churches as well as Christian organizations.
- Work for churches, missionary societies, and Christian institutions is more pleasing to God than other occupations.
- Unlike the work of evangelism and preaching, ordinary work does not have any eternal significance.

From a biblical point of view, many of these attitudes are wrong or inadequate. They run counter to the views of some of the most significant Christian thinkers and writers. They also run counter to practices that shaped many significant Christian movements down through the centuries. Today, in the wider community, voices have called for a rediscovery of the doctrine of vocation if public life is to regain its vitality and effectiveness. One of these, the influential sociologist Robert Bellah, argued that while

> we are moving to an ever-greater validation of the sacredness of the individual person . . . [that] is not balanced by any sense of the whole or concern for the common good . . . To make a real difference . . . [we need] a reappropriation of the idea of vocation or calling, a return in a new way to the idea of work as a

---

2. See "Millenials at Work."

contribution to the good of all and not merely as a means to one's own advancement.[3]

In the first section of what follows, we will look in turn at the biblical, theological, and historical bases for understanding and discerning our daily work as a divine vocation.

---

3. Bellah, *Habits of the Heart,* 287–88.

CHAPTER 1

Biblical Foundation

Work—From Genesis to Revelation

WORK IS TALKED ABOUT countless times throughout the Bible. It is present in the first chapters of Genesis and the last chapters of Revelation and most of the books in between. A list of the kinds of work mentioned in the book *All the Trades and Occupations of the Bible* runs to dozens and dozens of pages.[1] Some passages contain instruction about work, others present stories—both positive and negative—of people at work, and some simply refer to work in passing. We tend to think that the Bible's instruction about work is mainly concerned with what is done by people involved in full-time work of a publicly religious kind. This is not the case. Some passages in the Old Testament do focus on the responsibilities of religious leaders, priests, and prophets, and in the New Testament on the activities of Jesus' disciples and apostles. But others discuss or portray the everyday work or typical occupations of the day and the role of God's followers through them.

This is so from the very beginning. The first reference in the Bible to work people do is God's asking Adam and Eve to "work" and "care" for their environment (Gen 2:15). The work of the first couple is to be *gardeners*. This is presented as a divine obligation, in a setting God has designed, with a practical outcome springing from his concern that they will have food to sustain them (2:16). What comes from it is "good to eat and pleasing to the eye" (Gen 3:6). Indeed, as with God's prior work of creation, work is a not just good, but "very good" (Gen 1:31). It is only because the first humans

---

1. Lockyer, *All the Trades*.

break a prohibition about eating food from a particular tree that work will involve "painful toil," the obstruction of "thorns and thistles" producing "the sweat of your brow" (Gen 3:16–18).

The first descendants mentioned in the Bible are Cain and Abel. Cain works as a *shepherd* and Abel as a *farmer* (Gen 4:1). One received God's favor more than the other, but this is not based on the work they do. The work of later figures is described as *cattle-droving* (Gen 4:20) and *musicians* (4:21).

Biblical Portrayals of Work

Moving through the pages of the Old Testament we find more extensive stories of key people whose work was highly varied and contributed to God's purposes. There is only room to mention a few of these:

- *A Clan Leader.* Abraham played a seminal role in the history of Israel and indeed the whole divine-human drama. His role was to lead a large clan, a task that included preventing assimilation to surrounding peoples, and finding refuge for them when adversity struck (Gen 12–25).

- *A Prime Minister.* Joseph, the most junior of twelve brothers, was chosen to become the chief administrator of Egypt. In this capacity, he was not only able to improve the lives of the Egyptians but also of his people during a period of widespread famine (Gen 25–50).

- *Two Master-builders.* Bezalel and Oholiab were responsible for the building of the tabernacle. They were highly skilled architects, masons, metalworkers, and carpenters, whose abilities were described as a divine gift. They supervised a major building project designed for civic, educational, and religious uses (Exod 31:1–11; 35:30—36:2).

- *An Immigrant Worker.* Ruth, a young foreigner, took responsibility for her widowed mother-in-law on her return to Israel. As a consequence of this, she became a fieldworker on her uncle's estate. His subsequent proposal of marriage ultimately placed her in the line of descent that led to the birth of the Messiah (Ruth 1–4).

- *A Royal Consort.* Esther, though Jewish, won a beauty contest in a foreign land and became the wife of the king. She was drawn into a controversial and life-threatening political struggle, as a result of which she helped save her people from genocide (Esth 1–8).

- *Four Senior Bureaucrats.* Though exiled from their homeland, Daniel and his three friends become respected for their academic expertise, language abilities, and moral convictions. These ultimately helped them gain top-level positions in the Babylonian civil service (Dan 1–6).
- *A Civil Governor.* Nehemiah was a minor official in a foreign court. His deep concern for Jerusalem and its people led to his gaining royal assent to become its governor. There he displayed the ability and diplomacy to rebuild the city and establish cordial relations with its enemies (Neh 1–7).[2]

Some have argued that God's view of what work is important changed after the coming of Jesus. It is true that God no longer works through a nation to fulfill his wider purposes but through Jesus' followers scattered throughout the world. The main work of his apostles was to spread the gospel message in a very public way. But this was chiefly to be undertaken through the lives and work of ordinary Christians. To achieve this, however, they are never encouraged to view their work as simply a means to an end. It is through gaining respect for taking it seriously and undertaking it responsibly that they are to attract the attention and interest of others (Titus 2:9–10). As we shall see, the value of their work itself is also emphasized and its long-term effect foreshadowed.

Some of the ordinary Christians we come across in the New Testament are:

- *A Businesswoman.* Lydia was probably a widow who owned her own mobile textile business that had customers in various parts of Asia Minor. A devout Jewish woman, she became a Christian and immediately offered hospitality to others who responded to Paul's message (Acts 16:11–40).
- *A Fashion Designer.* Dorcas, or Tabitha, was a well-known local identity who had a high reputation for designing and making clothes. She was also renowned for her work as a generous benefactor of the poor (Acts 20:36–42).

---

2. Two other approaches to the biblical materials on this matter are Minear, "Work and Vocation in Scripture," and Stevens, *Work Matters*, throughout.

- *An Ethnic Leader.* Jason, the leader of an urban Jewish community, was responsible for looking after its welfare and extending hospitality to visitors. Though motivated by a strong commitment to God, it is best described in more everyday terms (Acts 17:5–9).

Several other early Christians with ordinary occupations became involved in more public Christian activities alongside, or sometimes through, their work. We describe such people as bivocational, even though most of their time is taken up with their everyday jobs. We also talk about them as "tentmakers," using a biblical term first applied to Paul. Some of these people were involved temporarily or part-time in Paul's missionary work:

- *Skilled Tradespeople.* Priscilla and Aquila were a married couple who operated a family business. Their specialty was tentmaking (Acts 18:1–4, 18–25). This was a mobile enterprise that allowed them to provide lodging for visiting missionaries like Paul, and oversee a small church in their home (Rom 16:3–5; 1 Cor 16:19–20; 2 Tim 4:18).
- *A Medical Doctor.* Luke was a doctor (Col 4:14) held in high regard in gentile social circles. On some occasions he was able to travel with and look after Paul and his team. He compiled a two-volume account of the rise of Christianity, from Jesus' birth to Paul's imprisonment in Rome (Luke-Acts), which displays a special interest in medical matters and needy people.
- *A Personal Secretary.* Mark was a younger person who had trained as a scribe. This work was composing personal letters for those who were illiterate and official documents for business or public purposes. He accompanied Barnabas and Paul to assist in their itinerant work (Acts 12:15; 13:5; 2 Tim 4:11).

Is There a Distinct Full-Time Work for God?

We tend to think that most of the key figures in the Bible were involved in public religious work in a full-time way. While at times they may have done this, mostly this is not the case. The following examples show that some of the time they were also involved in what we would call ordinary work as well. In the Old Testament, Moses was not just responsible for safeguarding Israel's relationship with God. The person more fully responsible for that was his brother, Aaron. Moses was actively involved in developing the nation's legal, social, and civic life, as well as its foreign relations and military involvements. It is similar with David. As well as being a ruler, he was a general and even the prime musician in the court. The prophet's task was to hold Israel accountable not only for its spiritual failings but its unjust practices, exploitation of the weak and poor, and self-centered lifestyle. The wise men mentioned in Proverbs and elsewhere mostly provided counsel on everyday family, community, and societal obligations. In fact, God is scarcely mentioned in their writing. All these figures are involved in matters beyond what are regarded as overtly or specifically religious activities.[3]

When we turn to the New Testament, while a small number of Jesus' followers travelled with him away from their usual family, work, and village, this was not the case for most. In fact,

> Jesus' followers came from all walks of life and many stayed in them. The first group, the disciples, included middle class fishermen with their own boats and servants. Fishing was one of the biggest businesses in Galilee—fish being the basic source of protein. Levi was a wealthy tax collector (Luke 5:20). To answer Jesus' call, they left behind relative wealth and security (Matt 4:18–22; Mark 1:4–20).
>
> The second group, the stay-at-home-supporters, followed Jesus closely and continuously, although they did not travel with him. They supported him and his disciples from their relatively well-off positions. These include Peter's mother-in-law (Mark 1:29–34); Lazarus (John 11:1) and his sisters Mary and Martha (Luke 10:38–42); and wealthy men like Joseph of Arimathea (Luke 23:50–51). This group included followers of Jesus who stayed in their occupations.

When we look at later figures like Paul, things are more complex than we tend to think:

> Paul was by one calling an apostle and by another calling a tentmaker because of the poverty of the church of the Corinthians, and because he would hereby stop the mouths of false apostles that would have accused him of taking advantage of the gospel.[4]

A study of Paul reveals that tentmaking was not just something he occasionally fell back on but a regular part of his apostolic work.[5]

---

3. On the connection between worship and work, see further Martin, *Workship 1*, and Martin, *Workship 2*.

4. Perkins, *Treatise of the Vocations*, 763A.

5. Hock, *Social Context*, 6.

How God Draws People into Their Work

We turn now from the ordinary occupations of key biblical figures to how God first drew them into their work. This involves looking at some of the key terms used to describe this process and several of the figures already discussed. The language of "call" or "calling" is the best place to begin.[6] This has been a central point of discussion from the earliest times to the present. Books from Genesis through to 2 Kings contain accounts of God directly challenging individuals like Abraham, Moses, and Samuel to do something for him. The major prophetic writings portray God asking "Whom will we send and who will go for us?," to which figures like Isaiah reply: "Here am I, send me!" (Isa 6:8). Prophets like Jeremiah and Jonah have a similar experience. The Gospels describe Jesus calling Peter and the other disciples to engage in his work (Matt 4:18–22). Acts records a dramatic encounter between the risen Jesus and Paul that describes his work, and Paul refers to himself as "called to be an apostle" (Rom 1:1; compare with Acts 9:1–9).

Down through the centuries, many have concluded that this is the main way God recruits people into his work. It may come through a sermon, a book, a biblical passage, a role model, or a congregation. Since few ordinary Christians have this kind of experience, they assume God does not have any particular work for them to do. This explains why many feel they are second-rate Christians in God's eyes, overshadowed by those with a call to "the ministry" or "mission field." Though they seek to do their work in a way that honors God and seek his help in doing that, they do not view their work as divine service or ministry.

When we examine words for "call" in the Bible, not just examples of people receiving a call, the first thing we notice is that it is used in a more general way. God "calls" all his people to respond to the message of the gospel and to live their lives in a way that is consistent with it. They can do this, says Paul, in the same family, work, and social setting they were in when the call came. Unlike some hyper-spiritual members of the church, there is no need to change their situation to fully serve God. If an opportunity arose to improve their situation (most slaves were actually offered freedom during their lifetime) they were at liberty to do so (1 Cor 7:20–24).

As the biblical commentator Gordon Fee explains,

> Paul means that by calling a person within a given situation, the situation itself is taken up in the call and this is sanctified to him or her. Similarly, by saving a person in that setting, Christ therefore

---

6. See Brown, "Calling," 1:275–76.

Biblical Foundation

assigned it to him/her as his/her place of living out life in Christ. Precisely because our lives are determined by God's call, not by our situation, we need to learn to continue there as those who are "before God." There let one serve the Lord . . . whether it be a marriage, singleness, in blue-and-white collar work, or socio-economic condition.[7]

This does not mean there were two classes of believers, those who experienced a dramatic call to full-time service in the church, religious organization, or mission field, and those who served him to the degree they could in their existing work situation. When Paul talks about the work most of his converts are doing, he uses the same words as for those who have experienced a direct call to a specific vocation. The word he uses for his work as an apostle is the same as he uses for the work of Christians in general. Both are engaged in "service" or "ministry"—which are simply alternative translations for the same Greek word—to God (Eph 6:5–9; Col 3:25–28). Paul similarly describes everything believers do, whether in the world or in the church, as "worship" of God (Rom 12:1–2).

The implication of this is that no kind of work is more "reverent" than any other, or that only certain kinds of work are "full-time" Christian service. From God's point of view, all are equally ministries and equally pleasing to him. Why, then, do some people have a direct "call" to what God wants them to do and others do not? In the first place, not all those involved in church or related work have experienced a call of this kind. When Paul is seeking a new member of his team in Timothy's home city, he finds out from the congregation who has proven themselves to be the most appropriate person for such work. He is the one who then invites Timothy to work with him (Acts 16:1–5).

In the Bible, those involved in more everyday occupations have a sense they are doing God's work even though they have not had any direct call to it. Return for a moment to some of the biblical figures mentioned earlier in the previous chapter.

The master-builders, Bezalel and Oholiab, were not drawn into their work as master-builders through a personal encounter with God. It was Moses who recruited them, after which they recruited others with similar gifts to assist them (Exod 36:2). Esther was persuaded to try and save her fellow Jews by her uncle Mordecai. Though she prayed for guidance, there is no mention of any overt divine response. Nevertheless, Esther was convinced she had "come to the kingdom for such a time as this" (Esth

---

7. Fee, *First Epistle to the Corinthans*, 306.

4:11). Daniel and his friends' foreign masters appointed them to significant positions in the civil service. Despite their unwillingness to engage in compulsory foreign practices, this was based on their excelling in civil service exams. Nehemiah prayed that God would open up the opportunity to return to Jerusalem and rebuild the city. Though he didn't receive any direct answer to his prayers, his sincere grief at the fate of his country prompted the king to agree to his wishes. Priscilla and Aquila were invited by Paul to join his team and, in turn, they had to persuade others in their family business to become part of the growing Christian community in their home.

As these examples demonstrate, God draws people into his divine work in a variety of ways. This does not mean that their work is inferior to those who experienced a more direct call. As our chief vocational director, God is not bound to only one way of guiding us into the work he wants us to do. In this, as in all his dealings with us, he is extremely versatile and seeks to work with our personalities, gifts, and interests.

The question remains, however: Why does God issue a direct call to some and not others? Why are some singled out in this way? A possible answer is that those whose work will involve directly calling others to respond to God are partly prepared for this by experiencing something similar themselves first of all. This is the main task of the Hebrew prophets, Jesus' disciples, and earliest apostles. As the well-known Chinese Christian leader Watchman Nee points out, even Peter, Paul, and John were not called in the same way. Each call is matched to the person's current work in a way that relates to the distinctive work God has in store for them:[8]

> Peter was called under circumstances quite different from Paul . . . and even from John, as we shall see. Since those circumstances are recorded for us in Scripture, we should not discount them as fortuitous. They are worthy of notice. Peter was called while engaged in the main skill of his trade, namely by "casting a net into the sea." The occupation seems (speaking figuratively) to have given character to his ministry throughout his life. First and foremost he was an evangelist: one who starts something by "taking men alive" . . .
>
> Where Peter initiated things, Paul's task was to construct. God entrusted to him in a special way the task of building His church . . . Paul comes onto the scene as a tentmaker, and under the direction of the Spirit of God . . . becomes, by God's sovereign grace, a builder of the house of God . . .

---

8. Nee, *What Shall This Man Do?*, 12.

Biblical Foundation

> The ministry of John is always restorative. He does not say anything startlingly new and original. He does not introduce anything further... [W]hat distinguishes John... is his concern to bring the people of God back into a position they have lost... Once more, this is in keeping with the circumstances of John's call to be a disciple... Like Peter, John was a fisherman, but unlike him he was not in the boat but on the shore of the lake at the moment of his call, and we are told that he and his brother were "mending their nets." When you set yourself to mend something, you seek to bring it back to its original condition... and that is the special ministry of John.[9]

Since the job descriptions of other biblical figures we have looked at do not involve calling in any direct way, there is no need for God to approach them this way. Closer inspection of their work, however, suggests that there is often a link between both their previous work and the means of calling them into what he now wants them to do. Bezalel and Oholiab were already exemplars of their trades when a larger opportunity to employ these was put before them. Esther was the king's consort when she was asked to put that relationship to a special cause. Nehemiah was already in a senior government position when he responded to a need that required a high level of leadership. Daniel was training for senior administrative work when more important responsibilities were given to him. This was also true of others we have looked at, like Mark, Dorcas, and Luke.

For others, being drawn into their most significant work was a by-product of their personal initiative. Joseph, and later Daniel, ended up in more significant positions through taking the risky initiative of interpreting important dreams. Nehemiah's plan for Jerusalem was granted through persuading his superior to agree, demonstrating an ability that was crucial to his later gaining support from nearby countries. Ruth's offer to help her mother-in-law and assist in the fields ultimately caught Boaz's attention and finally opened up an undreamt future for her.

In all these ways we see correlations between the tasks people are already doing and the way God engages them in the work that best serves his purposes. To understand the relationship between our work and his, however, we need to go beyond what the Bible says about our work and look at what it says about God's work. To do justice to this, we have to develop a more fully theological perspective on our topic.

---

9. Nee, *What Shall This Man Do?*, 12–18.

CHAPTER 2

Theological Perspective

God—The First and Model Worker

THE BIBLE NOT ONLY only presents an understanding of human work, but it also portrays God as a worker.[1] He is not initially described as Father or Lord but as Creator. The first thing it says about him is that he made the world and everything in it, including us. Only then does it go on to talk about the work we do. We tend to think that the kind of work God does is quite different from ours. But since we are made "in his image" (Gen 1:26), there must be some connection between the two. The first chapter in the Bible confirms this. The word it uses for God's making the world—in Hebrew *mlkh*—is the same as that used for human work. As Dorothy Sayers says, one of the main characteristics shared by God and humanity is "the desire and the ability to make things."[2]

To understand the link between our work and his, we must now look at what God does and how he does it. We can do this best by looking at the chief (i) characteristics, (ii) dimensions, (iii) descriptions, and (iv) purposes of God's work in the Bible. Much of this is indicated through picture language drawn from the world of human work. Some theologians dismiss this as simply God's way of accommodating our limited understanding. But unless there is some similarity between our work and God's, what the Bible says about him makes no sense.

---

1. For a full discussion of the relevant biblical passages, see my book *God the Worker*.
2. Sayers, *Mind of the Maker*, 22.

Theological Perspective

Characteristics of God's Work

We begin with the picture given us of God in Genesis 1 and 2. Although these chapters portray God's unique creation of a whole new world, people, and animals, they reveal something about aspects of work in general. When we look closely at what these verses say about how God did this, we find that work:

- involves both words and actions—giving instructions as well as making something (as when God both commands and creates living beings);
- means naming and making distinctions between things (such as between day and night);
- results in diversity, not uniformity (in God's case, various types of plants, species of animals, and gender differences, each with its own uniqueness);
- exhibits design and order (there is nothing random about what God does, and everything fits its intended purpose);
- has inbuilt rhythms—it follows a regular schedule and includes time off (God is described as following a daily routine that culminates in a day of rest);
- is a source of satisfaction and pleasure (God declares all he has made as "very good" and enjoys walking in the garden he has made).

When our work, if it is done well and for a good purpose, possesses one or more of these characteristics, we are doing something similar to what God does. This happens whenever we issue instructions, make something with our own hands, organize an activity, design an object or process, classify items into a list, invent a product and name it, add individual touches to what we do, work to a regular schedule, build in rest periods, and appreciate what we have done. In all these instances, there is something a little "divine" about our work.

Dimensions of God's Work

In the biblical account, God is portrayed as more than a Creator. Already in the earliest chapters of Genesis he is a Provider, supplying human creatures with clothes he has made and a garden he has established. It is not long before he appears as Revealer, Judge, Redeemer, and so on. Down through the centuries, theologians have described these in terms of the doctrines of God's Providence, Revelation, Justification, and Redemption. As we consider these, we begin to see greater connections between his work and ours.

Creator. This aspect of God's work is present throughout the Bible (see Job 38:4–7; Isa 40:12; Jer 31:27; Prov 8:22–31). While such passages mostly refer to God's creation of the world, sometimes they focus on his work of fashioning individual people (Ps 139:13–18). At other times they talk about the novel ways he shapes current events (Isa 43:8–19) or about his extraordinary cosmic plans for the future (Rev 21–22). Originality is also present in activities like sewing, cooking, flower-arranging, and gardening. It can be part of almost any activity. Homemakers, office workers, and factory employees also find ways of giving their work a creative touch. Their doing so is a testimony not only to the human, but also the divine, spirit at work.

Provider. In books like the Psalms, as well as in other biblical writings, God is often praised for the way he supplies the main necessities of life for both humans (Matt 6:11, 24–33) and animals (Pss 104:27–40; 136:5; 145:15–16). Every day we experience signs of God's ongoing provision— sunshine and rain, food and drink, safety and guidance. He not only sustains the world but constantly replenishes it.

This is reflected in many human occupations. We see it in the work of service providers, tradespeople, and retail suppliers. Those who keep organizations tidy, such as cleaners and janitors, and those who keep them running, such as managers and administrators, are further examples. So are taxi and bus drivers, mechanics and accountants, repairers and renovators. Environmentally, there is the work of gardeners, park rangers, and conservationists.

Even the most creative work involves some routine organization or maintenance. We should not chafe at this or see it as something inferior. It is simply part of doing the work properly. Some activities, such as housework, are largely made up of regular, everyday chores, but unless they are undertaken, life becomes messy and distracted. God himself has to engage in a lot of basic, repetitive work to keep the world going day after day.

Judge. God is deeply concerned with justice. He calls judges, prophets, and wise men, along with national and local leaders, to ensure this. While his justice goes beyond treating people fairly, and human justice often fails to live up to his standard, there is a connection between the two. This is why the apostle Paul describes those in authority, even when they do not believe in him, as "servants (or ministers) of God," when they reward people who do good and punish those who commit evil (Rom 12:4).

In modern society, legislators and government regulators, lawyers and judges, police and paralegal workers, are all involved in maintaining justice or redressing injustice. So too are social activists and investigative journalists, as well as advocates for minority groups and consumer protection. Any occupation that helps people receive equal treatment, challenges discrimination, and seeks conflict resolution is relevant here. At a broader level, any responsibility that requires the making of rules and dealing fairly with others contains an element of justice. Here we can add the role of parents with children, teachers with students, and referees in sports.

Revealer. The biblical writers constantly describe God as the one who reveals the truth. He "makes known" what was "hidden for long ages past" (Rom 16:25–26). Jesus describes himself as "the Way, the Truth and the Life" (John 14:6). The Holy Spirit is "the Spirit of truth" (John 16:13). In revealing the fundamental nature of God, ourselves, and the world, the Bible itself is an enduring product of this dimension of God's work.

At a human level, any kind of work that communicates aspects of the truth fits here. Those who provide insight into the meaning of life, personal relationships, the natural world, or past and present societies, do this—philosophers, sociologists, psychologists, scientists, historians, educators, and social commentators. Also, artists, poets, novelists, screenwriters, and playwrights. To differing degrees, limited by our human sinfulness, all these reflect traces of knowledge left by God in our consciences and in his creation (Rom 1:17). Anyone who accumulates wisdom about the way people and the world really operate is engaged in sharing something truthful. Whenever people have learned from achieving something worthwhile or through dealing with suffering and loss, their work falls into this category.

Redeemer. God's redemptive work lies at the heart of all that he does. It embraces what he has done in the past to bring about our salvation, what he is presently doing to persuade people to acknowledge and follow him, and what he will do in the future to fully restore the whole creation (Rom 8:19–22; Col 1:15–19).

What first comes to mind in thinking about how human beings reflect this is the work of evangelists, pastors, preachers, and missionaries. In a more limited way, it also embraces the work of doctors, nurses, and paramedics (who save lives and extend people's opportunity to hear the gospel), counselors, psychologists, therapists, and welfare workers (who put people in a position where they are more capable of responding to God), and those involved in conflict resolution, restorative justice, and conservationists (who seek to restore personal, social, and environmental systems). At an everyday level, any word uttered, feeling shared, or touch given that brings hope, expresses love, and opens up people to faith contains a redemptive element.

In all these and many other ways, then, we see potential connections between the work God does and the work we do.

Descriptions of God's Work

In many places, biblical writers describe God's work openly and directly in terms of human occupations. I have identified a number of these in my book on *God the Worker*, specifically naming God as Builder or Architect, Farmer, Fruitgrower and Winemaker, Gardener, Weaver, Clothes Designer, Potter, Metalworker, Composer, and Performer. Others we could add include Teacher, Advocate, Counselor, Friend, Guide, Warrior, Healer, Nurse, Writer, and Poet. Many of these recur throughout the Bible and throw light on aspects of God's many-sided purposes for his world.

The apostle Paul is a prime example of this. His letters are full of word pictures drawn from everyday occupations to describe the work God has given him. These include his experience as a tentmaker (Acts 18:3; 2 Cor 5:1–9) as well as the work of others in his day such as teachers, lawyers, ambassadors, laborers, nurses, soldiers, athletes, umpires, builders, bankers, potters, farmers, fruitgrowers, and businesspeople.[3]

This does not mean that the work God did and the work we do are exactly the same. God acts in ways that are both qualitatively and quantitatively larger, deeper, and more complex than anything we can do. However, our categories of work are built on what he does, restricted by our human imitations and flawed by our ingrained sinfulness. On the other hand, what we do is not simply an indirect reflection of what God does but one of the ways through which he actually achieves it. He draws us in as participants in his ongoing creative, providential, judicial, revelatory, and redemptive work in the world. In other words, he makes us collaborators in fulfilling his everyday and ultimate purposes.

---

3. See Banks, "Paul as a Theological Educator," and, more generally, Williams, *Paul's Metaphors*.

Theological Perspective

So, then,

> God gives us our daily bread through the vocations of the farmer, the miller, and the baker . . . God protects us through lawful magistrates. Vocation is, first of all, about how God works through human beings. In His providential care and governing of His creation, God chooses to distribute His gifts by means of ordinary people exercising their talents, which themselves are gifts of God. Thus, God heals by means of doctors, nurses, and other medical vocations. He makes our lives easier by means of inventors, scientists, and engineers. He creates beauty by means of artists, authors, and musicians. He gives us clothing, shelter, and other things we need by means of factory workers, construction contractors, and others who work with their hands. He cleans up after us by means of janitors and garbage collectors. God thus looms behind everyone who provides us with the goods or services that we need . . . This means that all work and all workers deserve honor. . . . In our vocations, we work side-by-side with God, as it were, taking part in his ceaseless creative activity and laboring with him as He providentially cares for His creation.[4]

As well as Worker, God is described as Father, Son, and Spirit. Liberal Christians sometimes focus more on the importance of the Father's creation and work in the world. Evangelicals often concentrate fairly exclusively on the redemptive work of Christ in people's souls. Charismatics generally highlight the Spirit's gifts and empowerment. However, since each member of the Trinity is involved in the work of the others, our work should reflect not just their individual but combined activities:

> So, while the Father is primary in creation, the Word/Son is involved (John 1.1; Col 1:15–20; Heb 1:5) and the Creator Spirit too (Gen 1:2; Ps 104:30: "You created all of them by your Spirit, and you gave life to the earth"). Christ is primary in relation to reconciliation and evangelism (Matt 28:20; 2 Cor 5:17–21), and the Spirit in transformation and completion of our relationships with God (Rom 5:1–8; Matt 22:37–40), humanity (Gal 5 and 1 Cor 12) and the earth (Rom 8:18–27). But they work together. Like the Trinity, we should all bless each one's work if we are to have a properly balanced work in creation, reconciliation and transformation. This is why we need a three-callings or three-commissions theology.[5]

---

4. Veith, "Vocation," 120–21.
5. Preece, "Calling," 5.

Purposes of God's Work

Let us now turn to the purposes of God's work so that we can appreciate better how our everyday work contributes to them. The first people were called by him to have families, grow in numbers, and cultivate the earth. Doing this, as many commentators suggest, involves not just agricultural but cultural development—artistic, technological, and institutional. God's so-called creation mandate, as Protestant theologians call it, is the divine charter for every aspect of human life, the Magna Carta of the whole human enterprise.[6]

This becomes clearer as men and women decide to reject his authority, go their own way, and break into competing nations. In response to this, while continuing to care about and sustain others, God focuses on developing one nation. Through a unique covenant he establishes with its people, they become bound to him and him to them. Israel's corporate vocation is to be the exemplar to surrounding nations of how to relate to him and embody his character and standards. God gives Israel laws to direct their life, prophets to keep the nation on track, and counselors to provide down-to-earth wisdom. He permits the people to appoint leaders, knowing that these are just as likely to lead them astray. He ensures that some leaders come from all classes of society so that no one group predominates. He also encourages groups of leaders at the local level, older men with proven experience, to deal with the specific challenges of everyday life.

To sustain and develop his world, God requires some to become farmers to cultivate the land, some traders to provide goods and other necessities, some judges to redress wrongs that result from human failure, some soldiers to defend the country from its enemies, some priests to serve temples and organize the annual festivals, and some musicians to celebrate births, marriages, and deaths. All these have their part to play or vocation to fulfill as citizens of this divinely appointed nation. Their work did not always take the form of a full-time occupation. A householder might act as a priest for a few weeks each year. A farmer could be a prophet for a period of his life. A king could develop into the nation's most celebrated composer. A woman might become a village matriarch, a judge, or an advocate and savior of her people.

When Israel fails to live up to God's purposes, he increasingly focuses on a smaller group of followers within it, occasionally drawing in

---

6. For a readable modern example of this, see Wolters, *Creation Regained*.

commendable individuals from another nation. This faithful remnant continues to play its God-given role in the nation even if the bulk of the people do not. This leads some prophets to foretell the coming of a figure who will do for the nation what it cannot do for itself. A few intimate a renewed future for Israel, the world, and the whole cosmos, beyond the present age. When the nation is defeated and exiled to a foreign country, God encourages his people to keep living in a way that reflects his values and purposes. They are to continue raising families, building houses, and cultivating gardens, as well as "seek the welfare" of their new country (Jer 20:4–8). On its return from exile, Israel is given another chance to give God its allegiance and represent his purposes.

When Israel again fails to live up to this, God's earlier promise to deliver his people from their faithlessness becomes a reality. The one who was foretold as their Savior turns out to be the Son of God. He not only appears but becomes one with his human creatures, embodying at last what it means to be fully in fellowship with God and to carry out his purposes. Jesus is portrayed not only as a Savior but a Restorer, as redeeming not only individuals but the whole universe. This involves more than just a return to the way things originally were and is the beginning of a new chapter in the story of God's relationship with his people and world.

Jesus' followers have the fuller assistance of God's Spirit in contributing to this. They are to share with others what God has done for them, and the quality of their lives, relationships, and work should point to the renewed world God has promised. A few are drawn into doing this in a more pubic way than others, but most undertake it through their normal family, work, social, and civic responsibilities. These are not only called to seek the conversion of individuals or to develop a new form of community but to bring about change in the wider society and world. The kernel of what every Christian does will not just pass away when this age comes to a close. Like our bodies, which will undergo miraculous transformation, so too will what is essential about our work, relationships, and care for the creation.

How Christian thinkers have developed these biblical ideas and metaphors down through the centuries will be the focus of our next chapter.

CHAPTER 3

Historical Development

Vocation—A Whole-Life View

THE VITAL CONNECTION BETWEEN God's work and ours has undergone considerable change from the first century to the present.

Work from Biblical Times to the Reformation

After the apostles, this began with a shift of emphasis in the way the Christian life was understood. There was a growing focus on the spirit at the expense of the body, the church at the expense of the world, and the sacred at the expense of the secular. This led to an increasing distinction between those Christians who were working in the church and the majority of Christians who were working in the world. A consequence of this is what the Catholic historian Aleaxandre Faivre calls "the emergence of the laity." In the New Testament all believers—including prophets, evangelists, and pastors—were part of the "laos," or "people," of God.[1] Only as ordaining people to a special status in the church replaced simply commissioning them to a task did a distinction develop between these two classes of Christians.

Clergy were regarded as having a special calling or vocation, whereas ordinary Christians, to whom the word *laity* was now restricted, simply needed to be obedient to God in their everyday responsibilities. As positions in the church multiplied, the idea of vocation was multiplied into a variety of church-related types of work. When monastic movements emerged

---

1. Faivre, *Emergence of the Laity*.

Historical Development

from the third century onwards, the word *vocation* was gradually applied to them as well. Though some of these movements acknowledged the value of manual labor, and initially some had lay members living in the world, attention increasingly focused on life in monasteries and convents. In the Middle Ages, even forms of everyday work were classified from the more to the less important. The leading Catholic thinker of the time, Thomas Aquinas, constructed a hierarchy of trades and occupations. Farmers were at the top and merchants at the bottom, but all were lower than the monk and those in even minor church positions.

It was against this backdrop that the Protestant Reformers recast not only the interpretation of Christ's work, or of work in the church, but of ordinary Christians' work as well. According to Martin Luther:

> It is pure invention that pope, bishops, priests and monks are called the spiritual estate, while princes, lords, artisans, and farmers are called the temporal estate. This is indeed a piece of deceit and hypocrisy. Yet no one need be intimidated by it, and for this reason: all Christians are truly of the spiritual estate, and there is no difference among them except that of office . . . It follows from this argument that there is no true, basic difference between laymen and priests, princes and bishops, between religious and secular, except for the sake of office and work, but not for the sake of status. They are all of the spiritual estate, and are truly priests, bishops, and popes. . . . We are all one body of Christ the Head, and all members one of another. Christ does not have two different bodies, one temporal, and the other spiritual. There is but one Head and one body. [So] There is no work better than another to please God to pour water, to wash dishes, to pick up the pieces.[2]

Similarly, consider the English Reformer William Tyndale:

> Moreover, put no difference between works; but whatsoever comes into thy hands that do, as time, place, and occasion gives, and as God hath put thee in degree, high or low. For as touching to please God, there is no work better than another. God looks not first on thy work as the world does, as though the beauty of the work pleased him as it does the world, or as though he had need of them. But God looks first on thy heart, what faith you have to his words, how you believe him, trust him, and how thou love him for his mercy that he has showed you . . .

---

2. Luther, "To the Christian Nobility," 265–66.

Transforming Daily Work into a Divine Vocation

> Now if you compare deed to deed, there is difference between washing of dishes, and preaching of the word of God; but as touching to please God, none at all...Let every man, of whatsoever craft or occupation he be of, whether brewer, baker, tailor, winemaker, merchant, or husbandman, refer his craft and occupation to the common wealth, and serve his brethren as he would do Christ himself.[3]

Similarly, hear the Swiss Reformer John Calvin:

> The Lord commands every one of us, in all the actions of life, to regard his vocation... Therefore... he has appointed to all their particular duties in different spheres of life. And that no one might rashly transgress the limits prescribed, he has styled such spheres of life vocations or callings. Every individual's line of life, therefore, is, as it were, a post assigned him by the Lord, that he may not wander about in uncertainty all his days. And so necessary is this distinction, that in his sight all our actions are estimated according to it... the principle and foundation of right conduct in every case is the vocation of the Lord, and that he who disregards it will never keep the right way in the duties of his station... [A]ll, in their respective spheres of life, will bear and surmount the inconveniences, cares, disappointments, and anxieties which befall them, when they shall be persuaded that every individual has his burden laid upon him by God. Hence also will arise peculiar consolation, since there will be no employment so mean and sordid (provided we follow our vocation) as not to appear truly respectable, and be deemed highly important in the sight of God.[4]

The main difference between Luther and Calvin was that the first had a more fixed view of the occupations available to people according to their place in the society of the day. Calvin was more aware of wider changes taking place in his time and had a more flexible attitude to people finding new forms of work and association. Both, however, understood the close connection between aspects of God's work and the ordinary work we do. According to Luther (who uses the word *offices* for our term *role*):

> Farmers, fishers, and men of all orders, who handle creation's wares, carry God's gifts to their neighbors, even if their purpose is not always to serve. God is active in this. There is a direct connection between God's work in creation and his work in these offices.

---

3. Tyndale, *Doctrinal Treatises and Introductions*, 133–34.
4. Calvin, *Institutes of the Christian Religion*, III.xxi.

Historical Development

> Silver and gold in the earth, growth in the creatures of the forests, the fruitfulness and unquenchable generosity of the soil, all is the ceaseless work of the God of creation, which goes forward through the labors of mankind . . . He who engages in the lowliness of his work performs God's work, be he lad or king. To give one's office proper care is not selfishness. Devotion to office is devotion to love, because it is by God's own ordering that the work of the office is always dedicated to the well-being of one's neighbor. Care for one's office is, in its very frame of reference on earth, participation in God's own care for human beings.[5]

Elsewhere Luther suggests that the ordinary worker has divine tools as much as the preacher or evangelist:

> If you are a manual laborer, you find that the Bible has been put into your workshop, into your hand, into your heart. It teaches and preaches how you should treat your neighbor. Just look at your tools—at your needle or thimble, your beer barrel, your goods, your scales, your yardstick or measure—and you will find this statement inscribed upon them. Everywhere you look, it stares at you. Nothing you handle every day is so tiny that it does not continually tell you this, if only you will listen . . . All this is continually crying out to you: "Friend, use me in your relations with your neighbor just as you would want your neighbor to use his property in his relations with you."[6]

From the Reformation to the Present

In the seventeenth century, Puritan thinkers developed a more comprehensive Calvinist view of work. The foremost of these was William Perkins. In a major work, *A Treatise on Vocation and Callings*, after expounding and systematizing key aspects of the Reformers' view, he spells out some of the challenges involved in seeing our daily work as part of our divine vocation. First, however, he affirms in the strongest terms that "Every person, of every degree, state, sex, or condition without exception, must have some personal and particular calling to walk in."[7] In fulfilling our calling at work, we should reflect God's character and values. In particular we must avoid

---

5. Cited in Wingren, *Christian's Calling*, 2.
6. Luther, "Commentary on the Sermon on the Mount," 21:237.
7. Perkins, *Treatise on Vocation and Callings*, 405a. On the Puritan approach to work and vocation, see also Stevens, *Playing Heaven*, 37–51.

greed or covetousness, being satisfied with having enough and not seeking more than we need. We must also avoid taking advantage of others. This is a temptation in every kind of work. For example, tradesmen who use false weights and gloss over poor workmanship, doctors who prescribe remedies without proper diagnosis, and salesmen who fail to mention hidden conditions in what they sell or employ deceptive ways of making money off of people. In all cases, the work we do must proceed out of faith and be directed toward love. It must be consonant with the word of God and accompanied by prayer. In pursuing our vocation, we must especially resist the seductions of ambition, envy, and impatience, ensure that we rest regularly, allow opportunity for recreational activities, and take time off when serious illness or problems occur. If on grounds of necessity we cannot continue one of our particular callings, or if we can do more good by altering these, we are free to do so. Though Perkins wrote in a previous century, what he has to say is still quite relevant.

Unfortunately, after this time, many Protestants began to place a greater emphasis on work, especially new forms of entrepreneurial enterprise. This, paralleled in the less personal religious perspective of eighteenth-century Deist writings, led to a gradual secularizing of attitudes to work. If before the Reformation everyday work was regarded as less divinely important, after the Reformation it started to develop an idolatrous character.[8] When, in the nineteenth century, the Evangelical Movement came on the scene, it heightened the importance of Christians engaging in evangelism and mission, and of work in the helping professions, yet tended to view ordinary occupations, though worthy, as secondary.

From the middle of the twentieth century, partly as a response to the physical and moral devastation of the Second World War, a series of initiatives appeared in different parts of the world that came to be known as the Faith-Work Movement.[9] This highlighted the connection between work and vocation, the importance of integrating Christian convictions and workplace practices, a discerning ethical response to working pressures and opportunities, and the development of a realistic spirituality of work. Contributors to this movement came from Protestant, Catholic, and more recently charismatic perspectives. While each display particular emphases—respectively on providing for others in a Christlike way, on

---

8. See especially Marshall, *Kind of Life*, on this development.
9. A full-length history of this movement may be found in Miller, *God at Work*.

co-creating with God, and on exercising the gifting of the Spirit—there has been a growing, though by no means complete, consensus among these.

Meanwhile, various Christian thinkers have taken a greater interest in the topic of work, including its role in vocation. In Protestant circles, the great twentieth-century theologian Karl Barth has also addressed the present-day challenges of vocation.[10] Unlike the Reformers who struggled against the narrowing of vocation by the church to mean "religious ministry," Barth wrote against the secular broadening of the idea into that of "personal career." For him, this is more about the human quest for significance than divine service, and about self-fulfillment than serving others, it also has to do with the rather feverish over-estimation of work as essential to being human. Barth argues that this ignores the fact that not all jobs are capable of providing personal significance, that unemployment is a reality for many people, and that sickness or disability can make regular work impossible.

Like his predecessors, Barth distinguishes between the general vocation to be a Christian and the unique vocation, or special place of responsibility, of each believer. This is something to be worked out through any and every aspect of life, not just through a particular activity. For most people, work has a central role to play, but our vocation can also include creating a garden, assisting a charity, playing a sport, caring for an invalid, and extending hospitality.

God has a particular mix of responsibilities for each person that he wants them to discover. They can only do this by "listening to his voice" as they go about their daily affairs. People's options will be partially limited by the period in which they live, the culture they grew up in, and the class in which they were born. These will also alter according to changing circumstances, developing maturity, increasing age, or occasionally more direct divine intervention.

In Catholic circles, a renewed interest in the centrality of ordinary Christians' everyday work was foreshadowed in the Second Vatican Council. This view was more strongly expressed by John Paul II's encyclical *On Human Labour* in 1981.[11] Some of the biblical basis for this—for example, making a great deal of Jesus' work as a carpenter, and the greater value

---

10. Barth, *Church Dogmatics* III.4, 595–647. Largely similar to Barth are the approaches of Brunner, *Divine Imperative*, 198–207, and Bonhoeffer, *Ethics*, 222–30.

11. For a helpful evaluation of this, see Preece, *Changing Work Values*, 199–231. Later Catholic writers on work and vocation include Michael Novak, John Haughey, Gregory Augustine Pierce, and Gideon Goosen.

given to employed over domestic work—is questionable. But in mainline Catholic thinking, the "active life" is now viewed as equally important as a life of contemplation.

The connection between human work and God's work occasionally comes to expression in subsequent writings by Catholic theologians. However, only work involved in major human achievements is talked about as signs of God's greatness and creativity. If, in contrast to Protestant approaches, they place greater emphasis on our co-creating—rather than our co-operating—with God, they rightly affirm the importance of seeing vocation as a communal, not just an individual, affair. Also, while they tend to have too idealistic a view of technology's role in creating the future, they do affirm the need to protect and care for our environment.

Though influenced by Barth, two important figures have mounted reservations about the doctrine of vocation, one from a theological and one from an empirical vantage point. Miroslav Volf has argued that viewing work primarily through the lens of vocation has tended to tie too much to specific class distinctions and economic structures. We need a more flexible approach that gives people more freedom to find their place in society and their most appropriate occupation. He concludes that the biblical idea of gift, or *charisma*, offers the best basis for doing this.[12] It is true that the language of gift was overlooked in earlier discussions, and that the Pauline language of gifts of the Spirit is both relevant to the world of work today and a corrective of current discussions about individual abilities. But this can be done by expanding our understanding of vocation rather than bypassing it.

The significant lay thinker Jacques Ellul points out that for many people work is just a necessity that dehumanizes and separates them from the results of their labor. For him, people often have little choice in the work they can do or when and where they can do it. In Ellul's view, the nature of modern work reduces even further the small degree of freedom experienced at work. This is due to its increasing dominance by technology and bureaucracy.[13] Ellul does find room for innovative Christian influence in other aspects of life, and his own work is a contrary case to the position he argues. He may also overestimate what he terms the totalitarian effects of certain tendencies in modern work. However, his concerns about the lack of choice regarding work in many places, and the effects of the mechanizing and bureaucratizing of work, must be taken seriously. Indeed, part of our

---

12. See Volf, *Work in the Spirit*.
13. Ellul, *Ethics of Freedom*, 447–81.

vocation at work is to counter them and prevent them from overwhelming us. Along with Ellul, others have urged that a vocational view of work should take the degree to which workplaces possess a sinfully broken and potentially oppressive, as well as secular, character. This would prevent Christians having idealistic views of work or overly optimistic hopes for reforming it.

Vocation as Involving more than Work

From the sixteenth century to the present day, there has been a recognition that God's purpose for us and our world was only partly fulfilled through our work. We need to look briefly at other ways this happens. Otherwise, we may fall into the trap of placing too much divine importance on work! It is not the only part of life connected to vocation. Luther and Calvin based their views on Paul's statement about God's calling us to reflect the gospel in everything we do (1 Cor 10:31). Puritan thinkers developed this into the view that our duty to family, church, and society were not just part of our divine vocation but specific callings in themselves.

Family. As we have seen, from the beginning God charges his people to have children and multiply (Gen 1:26 and see later Eph 3:17). This continues in the promised land and when they go into exile. Though God gifts and invites some individuals to be single, raising families is not just a biological necessity or personal choice, but a divine vocation. Undertaking it has both privileges and obligations that family members have to take seriously. Various members of the family have particular vocations within it—as grandparents, spouses, and children, and as aunts, uncles, and nieces—vocations that change over the course of time.

In a household, vocation applies not only to relationships but activities. Housework is simply another form of work. Though it is often looked down upon, partly because of its mundane and repetitive character, it is basic to a family's comfort, health, and quality of life. It also contributes significantly to the exercise of the provision and enjoyment of hospitality. If we think of homemaking more generally—the creation of an attractive, well-provided, caring, and restorative environment—this is even more the case.

Church. Another part of our responsibility is to fellow Christians. Serving God is not just something we do as individuals or members of families but as part of a group of God's people. We think of this mainly as attending services of worship and belonging to church organizations. In the early church, Christians met face to face in small groups to share and deepen their faith (Acts 20:6–12; 1 Cor 12–14) provide mutual care, and support each other's commitments at work and to society. Despite there being no differences of status in the church such as that introduced by ordination, members have different vocations flowing from their giftedness, experience, wisdom, and circumstances.

Today, many congregations encourage their members to spend a great deal of their time in church activities rather than equipping them to fulfill God's purposes through their everyday lives and responsibilities. Others acknowledge these are important but do not provide the support and equipping needed to undertake them. Since their members' situations vary so much, this is not easy. But small, face-to-face groups in the church, utilizing current resources on workplace challenges (such as this book), can do this effectively.

Society. We also have responsibilities as members of our society. This is an extension of God's command in both Old and New Testaments to "love your neighbor" (Lev 19:19; Matt 12:11). Our neighbor is not just the person who lives next door, our colleague at work, or a needy person we come across. Our neighbor is also our fellow citizen. Though our main citizenship is in heaven (Phil 3:20), we are also "*resident* aliens" on this earth (1 Pet 1:1). We are not just visitors or pilgrims here but have a dual citizenship. Like the Israelites in exile, we have an obligation to "seek the welfare of the city" and country in which God has placed us, partly because in so doing "you will find your welfare" (Jer 29:7).

It is not just our duty as citizens, but our divine vocation, to get along with (Rom 14:18), and "do good" to, other members of our society (Gal 6:10), sometimes joining voluntary groups working in a common cause. Once again, various people have particular vocations to fulfill. At a political level, voters, elected representatives, party leaders, or opposition critics are vocations that complement each other and can change as a result of the election process. We should respect and pray for those who are our political leaders (1 Tim 2:1–2), looking for ways of publicly addressing an issue or supporting a reform. We should take time to thoughtfully vote for the best candidates and some of us should consider running for public office. All this is part of our divine vocation and we are accountable to God for it.

Leisure. Although not all writers on vocation include rest, or leisure more broadly, this is one of its components, and there are strong grounds for including it. Rest is normally regarded as a-vocational, a break from work and other areas of responsibility. For God, it is more than this. Even though he does not need rest, God takes time to enjoy it and instructs us to follow his example (Gen 2:2–4; Exod 20:8–11; Deut 5:12–15). We should view rest, and restorative leisure, therefore, as part of our divine vocation, not just as a supplement to it. While we view this as something to take *after* our work is done, the early Christians viewed it as a necessary prelude to work, taking it on "the first day of the week" (Acts 20:7; 1 Cor 16:2) *before* the working week began.

Much has been written now on rest as necessary for our physical, psychological, and spiritual well-being. Sleep is a vital part of this. According to the Psalms, it is a "gift" that God gives to those he loves. If we regularly reduce it by "getting up early" so we can work more, our efforts will be "in vain" (Ps 127:1–2). They will not accomplish what we desire. Studies show that if people work too long and do not take sufficient rest, their work becomes increasingly less productive. Also, work that is driven by restlessness rather than rest, or restfulness, is less effective and harder on others. We need times when we don't have to do anything specific at all. Such spaces allow things that are going on inside us to surface, to sort out our priorities, and find the proper balance between our work, family, church, and civic responsibilities. We also need times to engage in leisure more broadly—going for walks, playing games, appreciating music, enjoying entertainment, and relaxing with others.[14] These are good for the spirit as well as the body. Christian leaders should model the importance of rest and leisure so that their people can see its importance, talk about ways can take time out—which is really time "in"—and not feel guilty about it.

Vocation, then, has to do not only with our work but with the whole of our lives. As Douglas Schuurman, a foremost writer on vocation who draws deeply on both Lutheran and Calvinist approaches, writes,

> All relational spheres—domestic, economic, cultural, political—are religiously and morally meaningful as divinely given means through which we respond obediently to the call of God to serve our neighbor in love.[15]

Our vocation at work has to do good not only with what is good for society but with God's mission for the world. For, viewed and undertaken

---

14. The best book on this subject is Heintzmann, *Leisure and Rest*, and for its connection with vocation see especially 208.

15. Schuurman, *Vocation*, 4–5.

Transforming Daily Work into a Divine Vocation

as a response to God's grace towards and within us, our work foreshadows the new world he is preparing.

In the next chapters, we will consider practical ways through which each of us can best evaluate how much we see and do our daily work as part of our divine vocation.

Part 2

What Difference Does Vocation Make?

Introduction

RATHER THAN DISCUSSING THE difference vocation makes in a general way, what follows is a range of job descriptions, journeys, and stories of people who turned their occupations into vocations in a significant way. It is important again to stress the difference between pursuing a career and developing a vocation. A vocation is governed by a more profound purpose and set of deeper values that often leads in surprising directions.

I will begin by providing a number of job descriptions that highlight distinguishing features of viewing work as a vocation. Then others will portray, in their own words, the work journeys of a range of people whose lives demonstrate vocation in a compelling way. To aid discernment, chapters 5 through 11 conclude with questions for consideration and discussion. In all cases, the character of these people's work is suggestive of what might be done in other fields of work. These examples focus on some kind of paid employment rather than work in the home or in a voluntary organization. They share the conviction that only if a vocational approach to work becomes the norm:

- can believers in the marketplace develop a holistic understanding of their faith rather than the compartmentalized one that tends to prevail;
- can churches properly equip their people for ministry in the world as well as in the church;

- can society benefit from the full impact of a Christian vision of work and overcome some current deep-seated workplace problems.

CHAPTER 4

Some Exemplary Job Descriptions

HERE ARE A FEW examples of how understanding our daily work as divine vocation can transform our occupations into something beyond the ordinary. These are drawn from real-life models, all but one of whom I know or have met.

Vocation has the capacity to turn a *mailman* delivering letters and parcels into someone who sees themselves:

- maintaining links between scattered families and friends,
- bearing gifts for special occasions from loving well-wishers,
- conveying information about services in the local community,
- helping to conduct business between suppliers and customers,
- creating bonds between people from different cultures and faiths.[1]

Our own local parcel delivery postman also greets us personally when we meet at the door to our apartment complex, informs us where it might be helpful what the weather and traffic is like, and goes the second mile by carrying our parcels up the stairs nearer our apartment door.

Discerning one's vocation assists a *maintenance worker* to appreciate their activities more profoundly as:

- cooperating with God's providential work by keeping his part of the world functioning in an orderly way,

---

1. Based on the influence of a mailman in a New York postal department who is commemorated on a wall plaque in words similar to those above.

- seeking to make working environments more efficient, convivial, and hospitable for employees and visitors,
- freeing others from worrying about material, mechanical, and technological problems so they can concentrate on their specific work,
- meeting half an hour before work each morning with Christian co-workers to pray for the day's tasks and those affected by them,
- regarding his work not just as a service to others but as a ministry to them.[2]

A genuine understanding of vocation can turn a *lawyer* from simply advising clients about the contents of the law into someone who is:

- a sensitive listener to deeper concerns that may lie beneath the specific issue they raise,
- a mediator for resolving difficult disputes between people before they get to the courtroom,
- a public spokesperson to protect manipulation of the law by wealthy people, large organizations, or governments,
- a donator of time and skill to members of the community who are too poor to seek their help.

Finding one's vocation can turn a *scriptwriter* into one who:

- is willing to devote up to ten years learning the craft and cultivating appropriate contacts,
- takes as much time as they need time to search out or create the best stories,
- strives to make all the dialogue and events as true to life as possible,
- seeks to weave seamlessly into the stories an element of faith, love, or hope,
- plots the story so that it is impossible for the studio to cut any scene without the whole episode falling apart.

---

2. This is drawn from the approach of a maintenance worker I came to know at Fuller Theological Seminary.

Some Exemplary Job Descriptions

A journey into vocation can turn a *business consultant* into a highly sought-after advisor to government, industry, and the voluntary sector, one committed to:

- a belief that a Christian view of reality provides the most credible explanation of the way things are and what they are capable of becoming,
- translating fundamental biblical ideas into practically relevant ideas and practices for the workplace,
- identifying the multiple and complex relationships between goals, values, systems, structures, methods, and culture in the workplace,
- recognizing the frequently overlooked role of design in all aspects of work,
- emphasizing the role of carefully prepared and inclusively led strategic conversations rather than top-down directives in dealing with workplace issues.[3]

An emphasis on vocation results in a *teacher* who has a profound impact upon their students,

- viewing education as, first and foremost, about helping students to learn best rather than supplying the best teaching,
- understanding education as not only about providing information but cultivating students' formation and societal reformation,
- appealing to students' imagination, since that is fundamental to their cognitive development, and providing opportunities for them to do what is being taught as only that completes their learning,
- creating a hospitable place for students so that they feel free to question and discuss as well as listen,
- realizing that you do not have all the answers and are willing to acknowledge your own biases and continue your own learning,
- knowing that, at its heart, teaching is an act of love through which students are wooed or courted to the truth rather than simply argued into it,
- recognizing that the best indicator of learning is how well the weakest or most disadvantaged students are progressing,

3. Based on the work of Tony Golsby-Smith, one of whose articles is "Second Road."

- developing the talents and skills of students that will help create the future world in which everyone lives.[4]

A focus on vocation can turn an *IT worker* into someone who:

- views their activities as, in a more limited sense, analogous to the Creator's work of bringing something into being out of nothing,
- decides to concentrate on products and services that are genuinely useful or life-enhancing rather than merely trivial distractions,
- complements their technical preoccupations during work hours with strong personal and interpersonal encounters to ensure their emotional and psychological maturing,
- acknowledges the fact that technology is not a neutral force dependent on people's moral choices but a reality that possesses independent power, generating further invention simply because it is possible,
- realizes that military uses of their inventions may be a byproduct to genuine national security,
- recognizes that some jobs will be lost because of ongoing technological advances and changes and dedicates time to helping such people find new forms of work.

A discovery of vocation can turn a *chief executive* from simply delivering a more profitable product or service into someone who:

- draws on the expertise of top designers to make furniture that is both beautifully and ergonomically crafted,
- fosters genuine community and just treatment among his colleagues and workers,
- creates a position of Vice-President for People and appoints a senior woman to it,
- educates and trains his employees in additional skills at the company's expense,
- appoints an architect to design buildings that enable every employee to have a direct view of God's creation while they work,

---

4. This draws on the writings and practice of well-known educationalist Parker J. Palmer, *Courage to Teach,* especially chapters 1 and 6.

Some Exemplary Job Descriptions

- encourages his workers' innovative ideas, provides resources to help them develop these, and gives them a share in financial rewards that come out of this,
- recognizes that the more you reach the top of an organization the more you are an amateur who is dependent on the skills and wisdom of those working with and for you.[5]

A sense of vocation can affect people in a wide variety of other occupations, but these give some indicators of the influence it can have. Understanding this can also help all of us to appreciate more clearly the contribution their work makes to us every day in the most detailed ways.

> When I go into a restaurant, the waitress who brings me my meal, the cook in the back who prepared it, the delivery men, the wholesalers, the workers in the food-processing factories, the butchers, the farmers, and everyone else in the economic food chain are all being used by God to give me this day my daily bread . . . God works through people, in their ordinary stations of life to which He has called them . . . In this way, He cares for everyone—Christian and non-Christian—whom He has given life . . . On the surface, we see an ordinary human face—our mother, the doctor, the teacher, the waitress, our pastor—but, beneath the appearances, God is ministering to us through them . . . When we live out our callings—as spouses, parents, children, employers, employees, citizens, and the rest—God is working through us.[6]

As a consequence: vocation is where sanctification happens as Christians grow spiritually in faith and in good works. Vocation is where evangelism happens as Christians teach their children and interact with nonbelievers. Vocation is where cultural influence happens as Christians take their places and live out their faith in every niche of society.[7]

---

5. A summary of several aspects of Max De Pree's approach may be found in Ledbetter et al., *Reviewing Leadership*, 69–71, 150–51, 157–59.
6. Veith, "Masks of God," paras. 1–5.
7. Veith, "Vocation," 130.

CHAPTER 5

A New-Settler Farmer

Cultivating and Resettling the Creation

COMING FROM A LONG *and distinguished line of clergy, after time in secular and pastoral work, Richard Begbie heeded the call of the land. He moved from Australia's largest city, with his wife Carla and three children, to a family farm in the hills near Canberra, the national capital. This became the base for a number of creative environmental initiatives. Many of his tales and reflections have appeared in* The Canberra Times, *and he has written several books, including a children's story and a highly regarded local history. Here he offers some reflections.*

In the thirty-mile arc around our nation's capital city are thousands of small farms occupied by new settlers. This is no isolated phenomenon. Most Australian cities and large towns have seen a similar growth over the past couple of decades. Urban middle-class people throughout the Western world have been migrating in droves to some kind of rural or semirural alternative. What lies behind this quiet pilgrimage? Is it middle-class indulgence or an eager search for the image in which we were made? What, if anything, has it done for the pilgrims? Answers can be found at many levels, and because they deal in the diverse and contrary stuff of human nature, explanations are both complex and contradictory.

Sociologists, demographers, and theologians look for common threads to suggest trends, tribal values, and spiritual meaning. But for the rural pilgrims themselves these generalities are usually less than satisfying. For those who have set out to discover a new (or is it very old?) relationship with creation, the answers that count arise from personal experience.

A New-Settler Farmer

That in turn depends on the attitudes and beliefs that inform the new life. For myself and my wife Carla, the change began a radical re-evaluation. I had never stayed on a farm overnight before we packed our few belongings and trundled from the inner city of our country's largest city into a new universe.

In fact, as a new settler I was a fraud. I had no real interest in country life. Our move was in response to a *call*, in the orthodox Protestant jargon of the day. The call was invariably to some overtly Christian ministry. This, although no one ever said so out loud, put the person who was called into a different category from ordinary Christians, who merely had jobs. Our call was to a ministry amongst young people, and for various reasons we had decided that the country would provide a good setting.

In fact, with the help of others, we did set up a community for young people. The experiences we had over seven years were formative for us all, though they won't come much into this story. My present interest lies more in the effect of the move on a well-educated, opinionated product of the sixties such as I was, a remote figure now in more ways than one. As our project unfolded, puzzling bells began to sound, quiet at first and then with such persistent clamor that even the self-assured young man was forced to pay attention. Instead of being merely a good backdrop for full-time ministry, farming began to insinuate itself as a way of life. The first hints of a revolution to stir my all-knowing complacency came with an exhilarating discovery.

I found that the simple activities of farming and stockwork, regulated by night and day, spring and high summer, touched my soul in a way I never expected. As Carla and our small child had done at once, I slowly began to sense my own homecoming in ways that I, so fluent with words and explanations, found hard to articulate, let alone understand.

I first became aware of it one evening in the fall, at that hour before dusk when the cool night air is beginning to settle in layers on the creek flats. The farming novice who knew so much had just finished his first day's plowing, and on a whim switched off the old Fordson and looked back over the newly turned ground. The steady diesel growl had left a deep silence in its wake, which somehow opened another dimension. The black soil was moist, still warm, a living organism with the mystery of new life pressed in every furrow. Satisfaction in work worth doing expanded into a sense of oneness with the rich granite earth, of a seemly and seamless fit.

It was not something I had sought or expected. In time I recognized a similar sense in a hundred experiences: in (for example) the intuitive co-operation of man and working dog or the aching limbs and home-brewed beer and easy talk around the stack after a day's hay-carting. It came with the physical delight of a meal homegrown and nurtured from seed to table, and it pierced the soul when my small child stabbed a wondering finger at the dawn sky: "Hey, look, Dad! The morning star!"

Later on, and more slowly, it emerged in the minor key, when lambs were stillborn and a bullock was slaughtered for rations. The smug confidence born of youth and a closed-system faith gave way to a new impulse—the urge to actually understand what was happening in our ancient new life, and how God was acting through it. This was a slower process still. It goes on as I write and will do so for a lifetime.

Paradoxically, it leads away from the idiosyncrasies that make our story different, toward discoveries familiar to most new settlers. Though life spins them into a single web, I shall try to tease out four kinds of relationships, devalued and often lost in an urban, techno-industrial society, but made possible in new ways on the farm. They are our relations to each other, to the land, to ourselves, and to God.

To Each Other

When we moved, with youthful condescension and urban wisdom we smiled at the older way of life we encountered, yet we understood little of the world of our new neighbors. In time we came to look beyond simple speech and quaint anachronisms to older, deeper patterns: a rich network of family and social relations, a scale of values that paid some heed to money and little to time as we measured it, and attitudes to the land that would take the urban cowboy a lifetime to unravel.

An early lesson in these values came with our first venture into livestock. The merino sheep, with its fine, soft wool, is well adapted to the grazing lands of our region. However, the merino needs careful management, including a "crutching" in late fall, when stained and dirty wool is shorn away from the sheep's crutch. We had no mechanically driven hand-piece, only a pair of hand shears known affectionately in the sheep country as "blades." At first, I enjoyed myself in the old woolshed, enveloped in the rich lanoline smell of the greasy wool. But after an hour my back was on fire and the spring in the blades had reduced my forearm to a throbbing pulp. After four hours I was near despair, with forty sheep done and sixty more to go.

It was about then that an old Land Rover appeared, driven by a neighbor. He had almost certainly measured my progress from afar, and knew I had no hope of finishing before dark. As long as I didn't think he was interfering, he offered a helping hand and we finished the rest of the sheep in an hour, and how that hour flew. As the last sheep disappeared into the yard my gratitude knew no bounds. "I enjoyed it," he said. "Anyhow, you'll do the same fer me some day."

By such easy steps we were we introduced to a framework of relationship that owed more to the New Testament than the ethos of individual rights and free enterprise. At the busy times of shearing and haymaking, in the emergencies of accident, fire, or flood, Frank's casual enactment of the second great commandment found endless variants and suggested new ways of relating.

Another kind of relationship emerged early on too. Two other neighbors, Max and Betty, would become the closest of friends, but before that, Max was my mentor. His entire life had unfolded in the valley. Interrupted only briefly by a simple homestead education, it consisted of farming the valley floor, running sheep in the forbidding ranges around, and preserving a family heritage rooted in that granite soil.

We were an unlikely pair, the voluble, well-educated, urban hick and his shy, stammering country guide. The simple matters of daily living for which a lifetime of education had failed to prepare me were second nature to the unassuming Max, who worked his way patiently through this alien's profound ignorance. Again, it was years before I understood the significance of his role as counselor, guide, and friend.

Then there were family relationships. Our children began to grow up removed from a society that devours without thought of true cost and consumes the trinkets of the age without understanding. And we grew with them. The children breached easily the watertight compartments of my urban mind: work was not a mysterious task undertaken by parents any more than play was a discrete activity for them. We all took part in both, according to strength and ability.

Tennis was something we all enjoyed, for example, but there would never be money for a tennis court, so we built one together. Sweat was produced in the building and then in the playing, but which was work and which play? Photographs of the hilarity and clowning that were a feature of the project make it hard to say.

The sense of being in it together also brought us naturally to the questions of role and gender that have convulsed society at large. Household chores, like most farm jobs, were shared from when the children were young. Off-farm income, important when wool prices are low, has mostly come from Carla's teaching work, and this has pushed the most inept of us into the full range of household duties. Her training as scientist and instinct as nurturer make her especially imaginative and thoughtful in farm-management decisions. So, the divisions in family authority and responsibility with which we grew up have been radically reshaped by our move to the real world.

Sadly, our arrival in the country coincided with the turn of the tide. Even as we began to glimpse and absorb these patterns they were disintegrating. The values shaping the urban world had already encroached far onto the rural fabric. Agribusiness was the buzz word of the day, and our neighbors were being told to get big or get out. Either alternative would shatter community ties and individual hearts, as so many were to discover.

The accumulated knowledge and shared history thus lost cannot be replaced by a degree or a welfare program. We, like others who cherish it, have tried to retain the continuity, the stability, the eager hospitality of that world. It finds reflection these days in our annual woolshed dance, where a mixed crowd of family, friends, and neighbors gathers for homegrown dancing, entertainment, and supper. To watch a new generation, bewildered at first without "professional" musicians and entertainers, gradually discover what ordinary people can do together, is to find real hope.

To the Land

In those early days I took pleasure in the edge given to the Bible's pastoral imagery by life on the farm. Isaiah's "sheep silent before her shearers," Hosea's "stubborn heifer," the hundreds of uses of the "sowing" and "reaping" images all came to life. Much later I realized that these were not just handy pictures for the Old Testament prophets, as well as for Jesus and Paul. These images were the deepest expression of an agrarian people's struggle to know the mind and nature of God. Their physical world would shape everything that came after.

A New-Settler Farmer

My brief moments of illumination had little to do with the knowledge I had brought from the education process. That dealt in neat answers, predictable quantities, and repeatable results. *Objective* and *scientific* were its favorite words, and I was eager to *know* farming in this sense. My mentor, Max, was confronted with a young man who wanted to add farming to his knowledge portfolio. My questions (and there were plenty) were all of the "How much?," "How many?," and "How soon?" variety. How much milk should we get from this cow? How many bales of alfalfa will this field produce? How long will it take us to break in this mare? How many lambs will we get from our hundred ewes? Max would look puzzled, and say little.

One evening as we rode home, my chatter and endless questions filling the dusk silence, he stopped abruptly and turned with his hand raised like a policeman to stem the flow. "It all depends," he said, and rode on. I barely paused: my neat economy of knowledge had room for a few variables. "Depends on what?" Then, in the half-light and to an all-knowing citizen of the globe, Max hesitantly began to unfold the contingent and unpredictable ways of God's world, which he had learned without ever leaving that hidden valley. And I, too, paused at last, catching a glimpse of another way of knowing. The illusions of a generation, an entire civilization, were exploded by Max's three words.

It depends on rain and warmth, on frost and wind, on temperament, on your neighbors, health, and climate change. It doesn't depend on your dad's income, or the stock market, or the weather forecaster, or the government. Dollars and schedules and income and GNP are merely props, constructs concealing the ultimate and true sources of our dependence.

With this epiphany came understanding of the great gulf that the celebrated American farmer-author Wendell Berry was later to write about, between exploiter and nurturer.[1] The one, with projections made according to calculator and ambitious profit margins, asks all the questions that Max endured. The nurturer or steward is more interested in the carrying capacity of the land than its maximum yield, in its health and that of the bodies and souls it sustains than in greater profit margins.

Max's revelation pointed to a value system that distinguishes the important and basic from the urgent and trivial. I heard about a wheat farmer who went to buy basketball shoes for his teenage son. He had to sell two tons of wheat to make the purchase: enough wheat for say 2,000 loaves of bread, in exchange for sport shoes that will last his growing son a season.

---

1. Berry, *Unsettling of America*, 39–48.

Modern society has lost even a meager cerebral understanding of "It all depends."

Closer to home, Carla has pointed out that of our 400 acres, about five around the homestead are devoted to our own supplies, namely fruit, vegetables, honey, meat, eggs, milk, butter, etc. Careful stewardship should enable us to grow enough timber for fuel and some building as well. The remainder, mostly light grazing country, supports the extras of a relatively modest Western lifestyle, and if we treat it unkindly it won't even do that. A true knowledge of our dependence brings a responsibility the affluent West has either expunged from memory or has chosen to ignore.

The knowledge into which I was initiated that evening doesn't just bring responsibility. It brings the sweet scent of new-mown hay, the steady rhythm of the morning milking, and the quiet arguments of chickens roosting at dusk. It brings the devastation of a lost crop or dead calf, the awesome power of fire and flood. There is pleasure in producing and satisfaction in the product. And as true knowledge increases, so does an awed wonder at the endless variety, the infinite permutations of the factors on which we all depend.

To Ourselves

Early in 1940, C. S. Lewis wrote to his brother, serving with the army in France. Warren Lewis had been a regular member of the Inklings, the informal group that met around his brother to talk, read aloud, and fraternize. He would have enjoyed news of that week's gathering, "an evening almost equally compounded of merriment, piety and literature."

In a laconic aside Lewis went on:

> The Inklings is now really very well provided, with Adam Fox as chaplain, you as army, Barfield as lawyer, Harvard as doctor—almost all the estates—except of course anyone who could actually produce a single necessity of life—a loaf, a boot, or a hut.[2]

In a more serious vein, Lewis often lamented his ineptitude in practical matters, and most new settlers, however adept with their hands, will all know something of that frustration. Because suddenly they discover the need for skills and ingenuity that (like Lewis) they suspect they don't have. The age of the specialist, we tend to feel, has freed us from all that. The

---

2. Lewis, *Letters of C. S. Lewis*, 176.

specialist can make or mend anything. When something goes wrong with the car, plumbing, or digestive system, our automatic response has become not "How do I fix it?," or even "What's wrong?," but "Who do I call?"

Some of the most vivid memories of our early days on the farm center on the waves of helplessness that engulfed us as we gazed at the burst water pipe, the inconsolable child, the laboring cow down and unable to deliver, the dead tractor. Was the phone working (often it wasn't), and who would come out anyway? We felt the helplessness of a race that has handed over to the specialist, and not just for microsurgery or genetic engineering, but for food, clothing, and shelter.

Like most new settlers, we learned from necessity. As we did, we began to take absurd pleasure in sheltering under a roof we'd pitched, eating our own produce, turning on the tap of a water supply we'd installed. Maybe it seemed absurd because we had not yet learned respect for the knowledge and experience that goes into sound building and wise stewardship of the earth. With our peers we had reduced that wisdom to dollars and cents.

As time went on, we gained confidence and discovered new abilities within ourselves. Carla, for example, had an uncanny way with broken machinery. The reclaiming of skills basic to survival brought a new sense, not only of control, but also of what can best be described as personhood. Backyard carpenters, home-spinners and weavers, and vegetable gardeners will often surprise themselves in the same way. What our era dismisses as merely a hobby is often a practical step towards restoring wholeness.

For the Christian, the reason for this serendipitous discovery is not hard to find. Each of us retains something of the image in which we were made, the image of a Creator. The echo of the creative spirit atrophies if it is not heeded, and the age of the specialist has done much to stifle it. Anything that reverses the process is a step towards our healing and re-fashioning in God's image.

To God

For years now we have been trying to re-establish trees on our overcleared grazing lands. Soil erosion, the need for shade and shelter, and especially the need to restore the diverse and robust ecosystems that once gave our tired soil its health, all make this project vital. However, it is a terrific struggle. What a few axe strokes achieved a century ago is bafflingly difficult to reverse. Every year a new insect, disease, or set of seasonal conditions brings some of our work undone. The further we delve into it, the more we realize we don't know.

The depth of our ignorance is clear to anyone who attempts a serious understanding of the natural world. For the Christian, ignorance challenges any facile or simplistic teaching of God as Creator. God does not, as the old saying claims, temper the wind to the shorn lamb. There appears to be as much caprice as good will, chaos as order in God's world.

On the other hand, there are intimations of something other, more glorious and powerful than we can bear. One scorching summer day I set out early to muster sheep in the ranges nearby. The dogs were keen, my stocky little mare fresh, and I was young and invincible. By high noon all that had changed. It was 100-plus degrees, we hadn't come across a sheep in hours of battling the thick scrub, and the water bottle in my saddlebag was empty.

With the weary farmer in a state of terminal exasperation, we suddenly broke into a small clearing high up on the range, empty apart from a single tree, the gnarled skeleton of an ancient eucalyptus. At eye level on a low limb, not twenty yards from us, perched a superb adult wedgetailed eagle. Did I pull the mare up or was she also transfixed by the vision? I only know that we stopped, with the dogs in our shade, gazing at the soaring monarch brought close and still.

The eagle returned our gaze and it was my heart that soared, as for a moment out of time it seemed possible for us to reach out and touch. How long did we sit, thus linked? Thirty seconds? Five minutes? I have no idea. Maybe eternal things are only possible outside our cramping measures of time. Then the eagle leaned forward, unfolded those mighty wings in slow motion, and flew with a rush of air from sight.

The passage from Isaiah came to mind, and our strength was indeed renewed: that afternoon we ran, and were not weary (Isa 40:31). But there was another passage too, on the edge of thought. Ah yes, "the creation waits with eager longing for the revealing of the sons of God." The "groaning in travail" of creation is a common enough experience, but the naturalist and hiker will gladly testify to these occasional moments of transcendence when that "eager longing" seems close to being satisfied (Rom 8:19–23).

If I had to single out the central hallmark of the new settler's experience, threading together all of these discoveries, it would be the profound sense of connectedness I experienced on that mountain. The family and community that works and plays together, firsthand contact with the real sources of human dependence, and growth towards personal wholeness in making and mending, all join in a seamless whole to connect the believer with family, friends, and God.

A footnote and I am done. You don't have to move to the country to work these things out. It took that upheaval to pierce my confident armor, but more alert people discover the important things in ordinary urban surroundings. My dawning recognition owed much to family memory of a suburban yard where my parents ran chickens and brewed compost alongside a vegetable patch, vines, and fruit trees. An old shed where boots were mended and furniture made should not be forgotten.

On the other hand, going rural guarantees nothing. A study I undertook some years ago revealed a whole class of new settlers whose primary interest is a more imposing yard and sweeping view.[3] Soil structure only becomes important when they go to excavate for their pool, and the shiny four-wheel drive wagon is for town display more than farm use. These settlers have successfully combined the worst of both worlds.

The vital message is that these discoveries be made: it does not matter much where.

Questions for Discussion

1. How would the farmer go about differentiating between the spiritual and secular part of his or her life?
2. What have we lost with the disintegration of older rural communities? Are those values and experiences recoverable in other contexts?
3. As we see from passages like Genesis 3:5; Isaiah 47:8, and Jeremiah 16:21, the Old Testament notion of knowledge is very different from ours. Has our perspective changed as a result of this shift in meaning?
4. Do you think there are any connections between firsthand responsibility for the things on which we depend and our relationship with God? If so, what are they, and how can we go about making them?

---

3. Begbie, "Move to the Land," 11–12.

CHAPTER 6

A Bank Manager

Reflecting Christ in the Financial Industry

SANDRA HERRON IS FOUNDING *Principal of MiddlEdge Inc., a management consultancy in Indianapolis. Prior to starting MiddlEdge Inc. in 2002, Sandra served for eleven years in the banking industry, where she pioneered her unique approach to organization development. She holds a business degree from the Kelley School of Business at Indiana University, an MA in Theology from Fuller Theological Seminary, and an Advanced Organization Development Certificate from DePaul University. Sandra is an experienced adult educator, trainer, and facilitator in academic, community, corporate, and ministry settings. She has always considered the marketplace her "mission field," and was at the forefront of the faith and work integration movement in the mid-1980s.*

The work of Christ traditionally refers to Jesus Christ's saving work as portrayed through three distinct offices or roles: prophet, priest, and king.

In his role as *prophet*, Jesus reveals God's saving purposes so that we might know the way of forgiveness that God has provided for us. Jesus does not speak on his own initiative, but brings the Father's message (John 12:49) and proclaims it to the people (Matt 4:17). Christ also foretells or predicts future events (Matt 24–25).

In his work as *king*, Christ restores his wandering sheep to their right path. He calls out of the world a people for himself (John 16:27), gives them a specific assignment (Matt 28:19–20), and provides them with varieties of gifts, ministries, and workings so that God's purposes might be accomplished (1 Cor 12:4–11). His grace and power are sufficient (2 Cor 12:9) to support us in temptation and suffering, and he overcomes all enemies (1 Cor 15:25).

In his role as *priest*, Jesus brings forgiveness and redemption. He offers himself up to God as the once-for-all sacrifice (Heb 10:10) so that we might be reconciled to God. He makes continual intercession for those who draw near to God through him (Heb 7:25).

Since Christ continues his ministry through us, our ministry can also be characterized by this threefold office. I find this model valuable in helping me discern ways in which my work is consistent with God's continuing work of revelation. As Robert Benne writes, "To make a comfortable living, to find work fulfilling, to perform a useful service to others, and to see all of this as participation in the loving intentions of God lights up the soul."[1]

In what follows, I will expand on the threefold office as it relates to my work as a Christian manager. While my language, illustrations, and questions are shaped by my recent roles as a bank vice president and service company department head, I offer them with the hope of stimulating reflection on how Christ may be made known through your own work.

The Manager as Prophet

The Greek word *prophetes* means one who speaks for a divine being and interprets his will to human beings. Biblical prophets were certain that God had spoken to them and that they were called to speak God's message.[2] The prophet

> is deeply involved in the life and death of his own nation. He speaks about the king and his idolatrous practices, prophets who say what they are paid to say, priests who fail to instruct the people in Yahweh's law, merchants who use false balances, judges who favor the rich and give no justice to the poor, greedy women who drive their husbands to evil practices so they can bask in luxury . . .
>
> Prophecy is not simply God's message to the present situation, but is intended primarily to show how that situation fits into his plan, how he will use it to judge and refine or comfort and encourage his people. Prophecy is God's message to the present in light of his ongoing redemptive purpose.[3]

---

1. Benne, *Ordinary Saints,* 165.
2. See further the call narratives in Isa 6:1–13; Jer 1:4–10; Ezek 1:1–28.
3. LaSor et al., *Old Testament Survey,* 305.

First, then, prophecy is speaking the right word at the right time. Prophets bring a word from the Lord to a particular place and in a particular manner. If we are to continue Christ's prophetic ministry in the workplace, we must be willing to challenge the *status quo* and envision a new reality that brings us closer to the values of the kingdom. In a competitive, dog-eat-dog marketplace, many will find this a difficult role to fulfill. Yet, when we question prevailing norms we most clearly see how Christ's work continues today in the workplace.

Let me give an example. In banking, as in many industries, there is a concept referred to as *differentiated service strategies*. In plain English, this means that different customers receive different levels of service. A bank's most profitable customers might be assigned a personal banking representative, be shown to a special (shorter) branch line, and be given special gifts or privileges throughout the year. Yet admonitions about the sin of partiality (Jas 2:7) cause me to question this generally accepted practice. Is preferential treatment for special groups of customers legitimate? If so, when does such treatment become unfairly discriminatory to others?

When I worked in the payroll industry, one of our competitors had a policy whereby set-up charges could be negotiated by the customer and salesperson. As a result, a customer with good negotiating skills might have paid nothing up-front, while another customer might have paid in four figures. To further complicate the process, the salesperson received 50 percent of the negotiated set-up charges, so there was a great incentive to collect as high a fee as possible. This practice of charging different prices to different customers for the same product or service is common in sales organizations, but few sales managers ever ask whether such a strategy is consistent with God's intentions and standards.

For the manager who prayerfully asks for the wisdom to raise the right issues, the questions are endless. How do I respond to a colleague who insists that there is no morality in pricing? How can I show special consideration for unique personal circumstances and still treat people fairly and impartially? Is shopping the competition an acceptable means of gathering market intelligence so that we might compete more aggressively?

When we raise these types of concerns, we are exercising a prophetic role. Unfortunately, a corporate prophet who questions existing policies and practices is rarely well received. Strong support and encouragement from a caring Christian community is critical for anyone who regularly finds himself or herself in such a role.

A Bank Manager

A second and critical component of the prophetic office is the ability to envision a new reality, for "where there is no vision the people perish" (Prov 29:18). I have found managers and co-workers much more receptive if, after questioning a routine procedure, I propose a creative alternative that can be easily integrated within our operation. So, when I criticize an incentive program, I also suggest a new plan that encourages teamwork and provides for a more equitable distribution of rewards.

This is where Christians can have a profound impact on the marketplace. The ability to see beyond what *is* and offer a dream of what *might be* is a gift. Most of us are so enslaved by time and economic pressures that we are unable or unwilling to step back and view things from a fresh perspective. There is a risk associated with putting on new glasses. The "way we have always done it" is familiar and safe, while the new way may be unknown and frightening.

The prophetic imperative also demands that we name the Name. As we fight for change, we have opportunities to share the gospel in ways that are sensible and appropriate for the circumstances. For example, when someone compliments the way in which I write performance reviews, I explain why it is so important to be honest with people, to help them understand their unique giftedness, and to enable them to become all they can be.

As a manager, I play a key role in helping to define my company's relationships with our employees, our customers, and the larger society. I have plenty of opportunities to integrate kingdom values into the corporate culture. My company is like most others. People spend a lot of time looking after their own psychological needs, delivering monologues on their opinions, guarding their turf, comparing their progress to that of others, trying to elevate their own status, and criticizing those who are different. In contrast, we are called to foster dialogue, affirm each other, value and promote diversity and dissenting voices, celebrate unity, appreciate potential, and encourage development. The prophet's role is to help people and organizations discover all that God intends for us to become.

The Manager as King

The vision of the prophet becomes reality through the kingly, or administrative, ministry. In ancient Israel, the king was viewed as God's representative charged with enforcing and embodying the covenant. Ideally, at least, he was a servant of the people. The king's primary responsibilities were to maintain peace within the kingdom by governing effectively and justly, and to protect his subjects from outside attack. If such an attack should occur, the king was prepared to oppose the enemy and subdue him.

Christ our King rules over all people and all creation. We can participate in that kingly ministry through faithful stewardship of God's *created* order. In my work, good stewardship has to do with managing physical resources—such as money, facilities, and technology—as well as ensuring that the gifts and talents of my employees are effectively utilized. Among other things, this requires being conservative in my budgeting and frugal in spending company money. I look for ways to avoid waste, such as making sure that machines and lights are turned off at night, reducing paperwork, and eliminating unnecessary reports. Our office participates in paper and aluminum recycling, and uses technology to operate more efficiently and improve the quality of our work.

The clearest link between my work and the kingly ministry of Jesus Christ is in my role as a manager of human resources. God has gifted each person with different capacities, ministries, and competencies (1 Cor 12:4–11), and when we come together as a body to work out the plan of God, we bring certain talents and abilities. This requires great care in allowing each team member the opportunity to exercise his or her unique gifts. Recruitment must be thoughtful, and assignments must be carefully divided.

The Bible contains some wonderful models of kingly (and queenly) ministry. For example, Nehemiah's strong leadership skills made it possible for God's purposes to be accomplished. When Nehemiah called upon the people of Jerusalem to rebuild the walls, he made sure everyone knew the goal and was committed to the work. Nehemiah's example helps us understand that the king's ability to make things happen is linked to his ability to build a sense of community.

Jesus Christ was the King of kings, yet he took on the nature of a servant to reveal the love of God and bring us into right relationship with our Creator. The kingdom of God is manifested in the workplace when a person in leadership takes on the nature of a *servant,* acting as a resource and enabler, and sometimes even as a protector from "enemy attacks" within the organization.

A Bank Manager

The Manager as Priest

In the Old Testament, priests were responsible for the conduct of worship, for the tabernacle or temple, and for all the sacrifices and festivals that pertained to religious life. Through atonement and intercession, the priests restored fellowship between a holy God and the sinful people.

Today, the crucified and risen Christ continually performs the work of a priest on our behalf. We continue his priestly ministry in the workplace when we point to his redemptive work and bear witness to his kingdom. When we care for others, celebrate with them, and try to serve as a model for them, we are fulfilling a priestly, or pastoral, office.

In most cases, business organizations are not easy places in which to exercise a priestly role. Some might argue that care, compassion, and love are not compatible with the drive for bottom-line results. Yet, as consumer expectations continue to increase, many companies are placing a greater emphasis on customer service. How ironic that customer satisfaction primarily depends upon caring and compassion, and is, in essence, love in action! When we ask our satisfied customers what they like about doing business with us, they say things like, "She really cared about me as a person," or "He made me feel like I was important and valuable." Our customers want to be treated as individuals and work with caring and responsive employees. And since, as customer service guru Karl Albrecht says, "The way your employees feel is ultimately the way your customers will feel,"[4] we must begin with the employees who serve those customers.

Care and compassion can and must be integrated with our drive for profitability. The entire management process must begin with the heart, not just because it is good business, but because it is right and consistent with God's intentions. As a manager, I try to be loving and supportive, rather than harsh or disinterested. I let employees know that I care about them as valuable and unique individuals because of who they are, not just what they do and contribute to our department. Even developing a training program to help our employees deal more effectively with irate customers and service problems could be considered a form of caring.[5]

We can call attention to God's presence in the workplace through acts of celebration. Our department places a high value on celebration both for personal and professional achievements. We remember birthdays and

---

4. Albrecht, *Only Thing That Matters*, 93.
5. See generally on this, Autry, *Love and Profit*.

rejoice in family additions. We celebrate new programs, successful programs, and completed programs. Once we even celebrated the "passing away" of a burdensome assignment to another area of the organization! Such rituals can somehow help us see linkages between God's reconciling action and everyday events in the workplace.

Our personal behavior can serve as a testimony to what God in Christ has done for us and to the presence of God in our lives. As part of the new creation in Christ, we can offer the hope of change to others who may be stuck or struggling. To encourage a trainee who finds it difficult to work with a particular manager, I can recount similar personal problems and outline the attitudes and behaviors I found helpful. To comfort an employee struggling with perfectionism and ambition, I can offer guidance gained from my own continuing battles.

Although I feel called to the mission field of business, occasionally I question whether and how my work is really contributing to building the kingdom of God. At these moments, God sometimes gives me a glimpse of his vision; I call these "kingdom breakthroughs."

At one time I was given responsibility for a new department and several additional employees. My predecessor in the job did not encourage employee participation, and I knew my first challenge would be to unleash the creativity of the staff and get them involved in setting our new direction and priorities. As I talked with one employee (whom I'll call Mary), I was painfully aware of how hard it was for her to offer any ideas. Finally, with great enthusiasm and dramatic gestures, I said, "Now, Mary, I want you to reach deep down inside. You're a very talented woman. If you had no time or financial constraints, what would you really like to do?" After a minute, she suggested a wonderful new program. I praised her creativity and asked for another proposal. Soon the ideas were flowing like a waterfall! As we concluded our meeting, she looked at me with great emotion and said, "No one has ever asked for my ideas before."

Missing Connections

Our churches, for the most part, remain preoccupied with programs and structures to equip lay Christians for the work of the church gathered rather than preparing us to be the church in the world. Rarely is work done outside the church recognized as valid ministry. The church gathered should equip us, empower us, send us, and hold us accountable for our unique ministries in the world. The church then can provide a place to gather and celebrate, be recognized and equipped, become empowered and sent back out again. There should be a rhythm of withdrawal from and return to the world, with the church acting not as an oasis, but more like a dispatch operation.

Though we may feel overwhelmed by this call and make excuses that we are inadequate for the task, like Moses, God can and will use us—wherever we work, live, and play—if only we will allow it. Perhaps this is the biggest obstacle of all. Are we really ready for Christ to be Lord over all areas of our lives and to face the implications for our work? Are we willing to deal with the inevitable conflict of values that occurs when we seek to apply biblical principles to our Monday-through-Friday agendas? Are we prepared to face ridicule and exploitation as we fulfill prophetic, priestly, and kingly roles in our institutions?

We know that the struggle between the old and new will continue until God brings about the fulfillment of his kingdom. In the meantime, as men and women of God, we are called to be kingdom-builders in the workplace and in every corner of the world. Although we may find ourselves in uncharted and unknown lands, we know that angels fight on our side and rejoice in our progress. And as we set out to conquer these new frontiers, we need each other to discover what it means to be part of the body of Christ in these places, so that we may press forward to reclaim every single square inch of creation for the glory of God.[6]

Questions for Discussion

1. Are you able to view your work as advancing the kingdom of God? In what ways do you, or could you, express the conviction that you are working for God?

2. How can the threefold office of Christ model help you uncover new ways of continuing Christ's ministry in your workplace?

3. What conflicts do you see between biblical principles and your workplace priorities?

---

6. For another fine example of a faith-based vocational approach to financial management, see Morgan, *Art of Loss Adjustment*.

4. Have you ever played the role of prophet in your workplace by challenging a policy that seemed inconsistent with kingdom values? With whom did you come into conflict?

5. Who are the most significant people in your life? Do you have role models from whom you can learn about changing your workplace to the glory of God?

CHAPTER 7

A Builder-Developer

Responsible Steward of God's Resources

PERRY BIGELOW HAS BEEN *a home builder in the Chicago area for nearly half a century. He has won national awards for building affordable homes and for his housing and economic development initiatives in the inner city. He is a member of various boards of directors and advisory councils, including the National Association of Home Builders and the Energy Efficient Building Association, as well as the Chicagoland Prison Fellowship, MidAmerica Leadership Foundation, and InterVarsity Christian Fellowship's Marketplace. He is also an adjunct professor at the Eastern College Graduate School of Business.*

For many years I had a very compartmentalized idea of faith and a highly secularized view of work. On the one hand, people needed to be saved, and I had a responsibility to witness to them. On the other hand, people were factors in capital investment and potential productivity, and I had to manage them to maximize my economic return. I became a master manipulator. I started the business to make money, not to build the capital base of God's kingdom. I even had the audacity to invite God to be my partner who would get a fair share for blessing me. I spent a lot of my spare time ensuring that I had a secure future by acquiring and growing my real estate investments, placing my confidence in these, rather than God. At the same time, I taught Sunday school, was the church trustee board chairman, and directed the construction of some of our church buildings. There was little connection between my Sunday faith and my Monday work.

What changed? Four things happened. First, God graciously used a severe depression in the housing industry to show me that there is no lasting or real security to be found in owning a business or owning investments. As a result, I developed a strong desire to know God better, to trust God more, and to feel loved by God. Second, just as this desire was intensifying, we studied Richard Foster's *Celebration of Discipline*. For the first time in my life, I began to practice seriously the spiritual disciplines of Bible study, meditation, and prayer, typically one-half hour to one hour in the morning, and fifteen to thirty minutes in the evening. Third, I read Charles Sheldon's book *In His Steps*, a story about a spiritually shallow pastor and his congregation and how their lives were revolutionized in one year by asking one simple question before anything they did: "What would Jesus do?" Fourth, I read Charles Colson's autobiographies, *Born Again* and *Life Sentence*, and was shamed by the realization that he was much closer to God after being a Christian for only a few years than I was after thirty years.

As a result of this confluence of events and intensive study of the Bible, I realized that it was spiritually dangerous to be economically rich (e.g., Jas 5:1–6; 1 Tim 6:9–10; Matt 19:16–26). I also realized that I had to make a choice between God and money (Matt 6:24). I became so horrified of the spiritual risk of being wealthy that I told God that if it was just the same with him, I'd like never to be rich as the risk was just too great. Before, I feared God and loved money: having decided to really love God I developed a healthy fear of money. I sold all my investments; I had nothing left except my house—no stocks, mutual funds, or other retirement-type accounts.

I also came to realize that Jesus deeply loved and showed proactive concern for the poor, so much so that in his story about who is allowed to enter the kingdom, it is only those who have directly and personally fed, clothed, and entertained the poor who will be welcomed (Matt 25:31–46). This was truly shocking because I didn't know any poor in my cloistered, affluent suburban lifestyle. I began looking for ways to touch Jesus by touching the poor. With the help of the Hebrew prophets, I began to understand how much God hates oppression and loves justice. Finally, I concluded that I was a *de facto* oppressor. I was not proactively *for* justice like God was; I was doing nothing to provide just opportunity for victims of structural oppression.

I toyed with the idea of closing the home-building business so that I could become heavily involved with the poor; ultimately, I decided to grow the home-building company as a means of support. I gathered around me highly competent leaders who could manage the business on a day-to-day basis. This has provided me with the financial support and the personal time necessary to become involved in a wide range of activities that come alongside people in the city, with those who want to help themselves.

My Basic Criterion: How Would Jesus Think and Do?

I continuously ask the question: What kind of a home-building company might Jesus establish and own?

I believe Jesus would build homes that satisfy a family's needs, not its luxuries. The homes would be of durable quality; they would have natural beauty, not status beauty; they would be resource-efficient to build and maintain; they would be designed to enhance family life; and they would provide the opportunity to develop interdependent, neighborly relationships. I believe Jesus would appeal to good, human qualities in his marketing; he would not appeal to greed, covetousness, status, pride, etc. He would honestly state the advantages of his homes. By the way, our commitment to be honest in advertising has consistently driven us to build better homes than our competition. Nobody wants to advertise that his home is average.

I believe Jesus, as the owner of the business, would pray the only prayer about wealth in the Bible: "Give me neither poverty nor riches, but give me only my daily bread. Otherwise, I may have too much and disown you and say, 'Who is the Lord?'" (Prov 30:8–9). A shortened version of this prayer is included in the prayer Jesus taught his disciples: "Give us today our daily bread" (Matt 6:11).

He would certainly follow his own advice about not storing up treasure for ourselves on earth but in heaven (Matt 6:19–20), not worrying about food or clothing for tomorrow (Matt 6:25–34), and not building bigger barns in which to hoard his Father's resources (Luke 12:16–21).

I believe Jesus would capitalize his business responsibly so that his employees could have steady employment. Following God's concern for more equal distribution of resources (2 Cor 8:13–14), the balance of his profits would be invested in helping the poor and spreading the gospel (1 Tim 6:17–19). He probably would not hoard, save, or invest profits outside the capital needs of the business (Luke 12:16–21). He would practice justice and equality in paying wages and sharing profit with employees (Col 4:1).

I am an entrepreneur, and I am a home-builder. I own and lead a suburban home-building company, and I am an entrepreneur in inner city activities involving housing as well as economic and human development activities in the inner city. I love to start things; I love to innovate. I am good at analyzing risk and future potential; I can handle the stress of risk-taking.

I am not, by nature, a good manager or organizer, so we have highly skilled leaders in each functional business area (marketing, design, construction, finance, purchasing) who are responsible for the day-to-day activities of the company. We meet weekly and make planning, personnel, policy, and procedural decisions by consensus. There is a high degree of camaraderie and mutual respect and, except for issues involving Christian ethics, I submit myself to the consensual process as do all the others. This consensual approach to leadership is partly a result of my understanding of my responsibility to be just and to foster equality. Even though some of the leaders are not believers, this group has been able to provide mutual accountability. This consensual approach provides what Max DePree calls the "space . . . to exercise our gifts and diversity."[1]

The biblical model for co-participation and fellowship is the body (Rom 12:3–8; 1 Cor 12:4–29). So long as people are committed to a common goal, the body is a better metaphor for business organization than the typical hierarchical organization chart. There is still hierarchy but it is interdependence, collaboration, and consensus that are emphasized. This body metaphor and consensual interdependence pervades the relationships within each operating area and across all areas of the company. There are no private kingdoms in our company; no one builds moats or gates, and no one is a gatekeeper. Each person's work is integrated and interrelated with the work of others, and there is a high level of respect for each person's contribution.

A person's dignity and self-esteem will not be enhanced by their work unless they can see how their work either directly or indirectly results in the production and distribution of a quality product or service. Therefore, a highly visible trail between an employee's work, the home we build, and the purchaser of that home must be evident. This trail is made visible through the human inter-relationships involved in each person's contribution. Our broad-based mutual accountability and inter-relatedness results in a culture that develops strong, independent people with a high level of mutual self-respect. It is a satisfying culture within which to work. One of our leaders often says he has the best of all worlds: he loves to come to work in the morning, and he loves to go home at night! It is not unusual to have

---

1. De Pree, *Leadership Is an Art*, 7, 14.

a first-time visitor to our office say something like "It's so peaceful here; everyone is so content."

We feel that we have a responsibility to provide steady employment. This is very difficult to do since the home-building industry is extremely cyclical. It is not unusual for housing starts in a given market to drop by 60 to 80 percent in a short time. We have a threefold strategy to stabilize employment. First, we invest heavily in information systems that result in very high individual productivity. Second, in good times we do not expand as rapidly as we could. Third, we have no goal to be big for the sake of being big. We aim for careful, sustainable growth.

This combination allowed us to go through the last housing cycle without laying off anyone, while many home-builders were reducing their staffs by 50 to 70 percent.

Because we recognize that a person who joins our firm must operate within the business culture we have created, we take the interviewing process very seriously. We want to make sure that new employees will fit well with our group and have full knowledge of our approach to business, so that they can make good decisions as to whether they will enjoy working with us. This process involves several meetings and usually stretches over several weeks. By the time they are hired, new employees feel like they are known, that they are respected for their skills, that both strengths and weaknesses have been acknowledged, and that they will be treated with dignity and respect. All full-time employees go through the same interview process, whether to become a vice-president or a receptionist.

Our people are so important to us that no personnel decision is made until there is full consensus by the leadership group. Every employee is told that the owner of the company operates the company on basic biblical principles, which means that the truth will always be spoken in love (Eph 4:15) and that we shall never knowingly lie to each other, a home buyer, a supplier or subcontractor, or government official. We place a high premium on personal integrity, and we want potential employees to know that they will not enjoy working with us if they do not have what Stephen Covey calls the character ethic of integrity and principle-centered leadership.[2] One of the results of this fastidious honesty is that over time people outside our company have come to trust our employees implicitly.

We use biblical principles of body interdependence and *koinonia* (fellowship and co-participation) in the design of our communities. In his

---

2. Covey, *Principle-Centered Leadership*.

book *Habits of the Heart,* Robert Bellah has observed that there must be a careful balance between individualism and interdependence to maintain democratic, neighborly oriented lifestyles.[3] Suburban communities have lost that balance; they have become extremely individualistic. The way builders relate homes to the street and each other today almost precludes the development of natural neighborliness between families. Our communities restore a balance between privacy and neighborliness, and they result in natural opportunities to interact in a neighborly way.

In the 1990s, we received a national reputation for building innovative, highly energy-efficient homes, with a guarantee that the heating bills would not exceed $200 per year. Our innovation in energy efficiency is a direct result of our great respect for God's creation and a belief that we should preserve as much of it as we can for our children's children. We strive to preserve the natural beauty of land as we plan and develop it. I do not see how a believer can be anything other than an environmentalist; it is only responsible stewardship to cherish and respect what God graciously has given us.

Our Work in the Inner City

I enjoy my work in the inner city as much as my work in the suburbs. You could say that we make money in the suburbs and spend it in the inner city. I became deeply involved in working with economically poor people in the inner city by asking these questions: What would Jesus do? Where would Jesus invest or spend his Father's resources? How would Jesus practice equality? Where would Jesus live?

I moved to an African-American community in Chicago's inner city, and my home church is predominantly African American. Originally, I became involved because Jesus called me, not because I wanted to. In hindsight, as a result of the joy of the work I do and the joy of where I live and worship, I would do it now for the joy because of the rich relationships I have. I am loved, nurtured, and cared about there. I am not saying that all believers should live among the economically poor; however, it does seem odd that the vast preponderance of those who have an economic choice and who have Jesus in their hearts ask only the question: "Where amongst the rich should I live?" instead of "Where amongst *all* of God's people does he want me to live?"

3. Bellah, *Habits of the Heart*, especially chapter 3.

A Builder-Developer

There is not enough space here to develop fully the biblical presuppositions surrounding my work and life in the inner city. However, I would like to briefly explain these and the work I do. The biblical presuppositions are as follows:

Jubilee. God instituted an economic system in Israel that was designed to provide an even distribution of the economic resources necessary to live a godly life. Although Jubilee rewarded industriousness and penalized laziness, there was no way individuals could become excessively and extravagantly wealthy. Part of the plan was a redistribution system preventing any family from becoming permanently impoverished due to economic adversity or individual laziness (Deut 15; Lev 25:8–43). Jesus extended this principle further, involving a degree of giving and sharing that can only be fully actualized in kingdom relationships.

Equality. Paul encouraged the churches to practice economic equality (2 Cor 8:1—9:15). Those who have God's resources are to share so thoroughly and deeply that they run the risk of becoming impoverished themselves (2 Cor 8:14) as Jesus did (2 Cor 8:9).

Calling. God has provided a "good work" for every believer to do (Eph 2:10). Unfortunately, many people have been deprived of the capital, training, and personal resources necessary to accomplish that good work. Those of us who are stewards of God's resources must make sure that they are fully shared and that all believers have the opportunity and resources to do the good work God has called them to do.

Gleaning. The principle of gleaning involves providing others with the opportunity to help themselves. In Israel, able-bodied people were to be given the opportunity to provide for themselves from what others produced. The story of Ruth and Boaz is the perfect example of this principle at work.

Justice. God loves justice and hates oppression (Isa 58; Amos 5; Jas 5:1–6). I used to see myself as a self-made individualist, having come from an economically poor background. I forgot about a loving father who, by his example, instilled in me a positive attitude of hope; a mother who deeply loved God; an older sister who deeply loved me; a brother who counseled me; innumerable friends who stood by me; people who mentored me; and a country of opportunity, a superb educational system, etc. I selected almost none of these; they are all gifts of God through others' investments in me. Except for these opportunities (over which I had no control) I'd be among the poorest of the poor, both spiritually and physically.

God says: Invest in the poor as I have invested in you. I am God's steward of those investments, of those good works. When I see all that I am and have as God's gift and stewardship, and when I hear God shout jubilee, grace, equality, sharing, and justice, I cannot claim any of that wealth for my own; the entrepreneurial and building skills, the networking and financial resources, all are God's to be shared fully with others. It is helping others help themselves so they can help others, just as others helped me so I could help others.

I am participating in the cycle of reinvestment and helping to stop the cycle of disinvestment in the inner city. I use investment and reinvestment in the broadest sense to include spiritual, economic, social, institutional, and moral concerns, as well as personal time, mentoring, youth development, business and professional networks, technical skills, and any other kind of investment you can imagine. We have the ability and the perseverance to be "seed hope" and "seed capital" to see an opportunity through to completion.

Everything we are involved in in the inner city is a joint venture or partnership with either a church or a church-related community development group. We do nothing by ourselves. We help low-income, working people build their own high-quality, energy-efficient homes. We provide organizational expertise, seed capital, hope, technical design, construction management, land development, risk-taking and entrepreneurial skills, purchasing networks, and financial resources, but the people are building the homes themselves. We coordinate the efforts of people from all walks of life: accountants, carpenters, lawyers, electricians, business owners, plumbers, and truck drivers. Our objective is to make kingdom resources available to kingdom people.

I make all of the resources of the suburban home-building company available to the work being done in the inner city, except for the employees themselves. Inner city work is not, and cannot be, a condition of employment for the employees, many of whom are not believers. However, all of the business networks, technical skills, knowledge, and financial resources are fully available to be shared.

Conclusion

I walk down life's path continually asking the questions: How would Jesus think? What would Jesus do? I know that I am the workmanship of God

A Builder-Developer

and that he has provided a whole range of good work for me to do. All of the good work I do is blessed and is a blessing to me and to others, whether it is designing and building homes and neighborhoods in the suburbs or recapitalizing and rebuilding the inner city, whether it is respecting the image of God and the incarnation of Jesus in an employee, customer, or friend or mentoring and modeling Jesus' incarnation in decaying urban centers. It is the highest joy and honor to give back to Jesus as much as I can of what he has given to me.

Questions for Discussion

1. How could applying the principle of offering others "God's gift of making decisions" change one's approach to their work?

2. In what ways has the desire to accumulate wealth influenced your spiritual choices? If you were to change your attitudes about wealth, how would that affect your role in the workplace (See Jas 2:5–7; 5:1–6; 1 Tim 6:9–10; Matt 6:24; 19:16–26)?

3. How would your work be changed if you asked yourself: "What would Jesus think and what would Jesus do?" before making your decisions?

4. How could you apply the biblical principles of jubilee, equality, calling, gleaning, and justice to your present work?

CHAPTER 8

A Business Owner

Christian Mission in a Car Sales Firm

Don Flow is a well-known entrepreneur and chairman and CEO of the Flow Automotive Companies, operating around three dozen dealerships in the United States. He also serves on a number of civic, organizational, and educational boards, and is an elder in a Presbyterian church. Having undertaken a diploma in Christian Studies at Regent College, Vancouver, he has worked closely with R. Paul Stevens in a number of Marketplace Theological courses and been involved in several Christian Marketplace initiatives.

What follows is an outgrowth of my own personal quest, a quest for which I have great passion: To have my faith transform my work. I have attempted to develop a biblical perspective as the foundation for understanding my life in the marketplace and a coherent worldview that can be articulated in a workplace setting. From this framework I have derived relevant managerial and organizational principles for my automobile dealerships.

The Threefold Call of Christ

The call of Christ is the most profound event in human experience—it is regenerating, redefining, and refocusing. This call has three dimensions—to *salvation*, to *sanctification*, and to *service*. It is not a call to leave the world behind to live the life of faith, but rather to live the life of faith in the midst of the world. In every sphere of life, we must work out that call. And that threefold call must be held together as a unity. When the call is fractured, with one dimension being the single focus, we will live a truncated, fragmented life. When reduced to salvation only, the call easily becomes "believe-ism," like the rush of adrenaline that has little impact on our character or relationships. When the call by Christ is reduced to sanctification, it is diminished to moralism, which is not an outgrowth of grace and tends to become self-righteous. When reduced to service, the call of Christ easily becomes activism, no longer energized by the inner renewal of the Holy Spirit but driven by our need to do something significant.

Our call comes in a specific personal place, in a particular culture, with a defined sphere of relationships, and with certain desires and preferences. When Christ calls us, we are restored and renewed to what we were *meant* to be rather than just an improved edition of who we *used* to be. Like Saul of Tarsus, Jesus gives us a new name, one that gives ultimate purpose and meaning to our existence—communion with God, community with one another, and co-creation with God in the world (2 Cor 5:17–20). We will never know in advance exactly where the call of Christ will lead us in our journey.

Governing Commitments

Bringing definition to our call or making it real for a specific place in life means responding to three profound questions. Why? What? How? The response to these three questions leads to what I call the governing commitments in our life.

The answer to why is the purpose or reason for our existence. The answer to the question of what is vision—the picture of the future we seek to create. While purpose and mission represent a direction, vision leads to a specific destination. Purpose is at the foundation of our being. Vision wells up from within us and finds expression in the specifics of life. Purpose is abstract, vision is concrete. A vision with no underlying sense of purpose cannot be sustained because it fails to address fundamental reasons for existence. Our core values define how we will act and live as we pursue our vision. My vision brings definition to my call in a particular place, and my core values are the point of tangible integration.

These governing commitments are also applicable to organizations. I have implemented the governing commitments in my car dealerships and have found that the explicit recognition and integration of purpose, vision, and core values must take place for an organization to flourish. Focusing on the governing commitments of organizational life forces us together to answer "What do we believe?" The energy that comes when an organization commits to a purpose, vision, and core values derives from the power of these governing commitments to fulfill intrinsic desires for meaning that transcend specific economic goals. These desires have the power to call forth a level of commitment and dedication that creates a common identity among diverse people.

My personal workplace vision statement, what I want to be, is not a final statement: my identity before God is not static and the circumstances in which he has placed me are always evolving. This statement runs:

> To articulate and embody a vision of our organization as a community of uniquely gifted people whose life together is characterized by grace and truth and whose reason for existence is to serve others.

In this statement are three core values that bear witness to Jesus Christ, the point of integration in my work life and how my calling takes on real meaning. These three values are: extraordinary service to others, the development of people, and community building.

Extraordinary Service to Others

Extraordinary service to others is consonant with the words of Jesus: "Whoever wants to become great among you must be your servant, just as the Son of Man did not come to be served, but to serve" (Matt 20:26-28). If the primary character attribute of Jesus was that of service, then this characteristic should dominate my behavior as well. As the president of the company, it is my goal that this be the defining attribute of the entire organization. Since this goal is the very foundation of our existence, it is captured in our company's mission statement: "To deliver an extraordinary level of service at every point of contact with the customer in a personal and professional manner."

We debated and agonized over every word in this statement. One of the benefits of being the owner of a company is that there is great opportunity for congruence between personal governing commitments and corporate governing commitments. Nonetheless, ownership of the capital does not imply ownership of the mission. For a corporate mission to be a living reality, it must be fully integrated into the organizational culture. The mission statement creates the foundation for developing the shared vision of our company. To make this vision a reality, there must be a common language that conveys the emotive dimension of the vision. Development of that common language is my responsibility.

To accomplish this, I meet with employees daily, one-on-one and in groups. I ask them how I can help them fulfill our vision. Our common language includes words and phrases such as: exceeding customers' expectations, going the extra mile, giving of ourselves, being there for our customers, building trust, developing relationships, serving when it is not convenient, and creating customer enthusiasm.

In addition, we define our success in how we have served our customers. We survey customers after they have purchased vehicles or received service. Roughly one-third of our employees' compensation depends on customers' perceptions of service. We think that declaring our intentions to the customer is important because that holds us accountable to the vision. Once we have declared our standards, they provide the norm for defining our progress towards the vision.

One of the ways we declare standards to ourselves and to our customers is to post our commitments throughout the dealerships. We review with every customer our promise to them. For instance, in our service departments, we have a commitment board that is prominently positioned for every customer to read. It states:

Our Commitment to You!

1. To properly diagnose and repair your vehicle on the first visit to the dealership. If we fail to do so, we will provide you with substitute transportation. We will return your vehicle to you totally cleaned and vacuumed.

2. To provide you with an estimate before we begin the repairs on your car. If we fail to do so, we will repair your car at no charge.

3. To repair your vehicle for the price promised. If we exceed the amount you authorize, we will pay for it. No questions asked.

4. To complete your repairs when we promise. If we fail to do so, we will provide you with transportation while we finish the repairs.

These are just a few of the examples of our efforts to strive to make our vision a reality today.

Beyond communicating the vision verbally, as the leader of the company it is my responsibility to incarnate or embody the vision. I must set the example through my behavior. I must be willing to see myself as the servant of the organization. What this means is that the members of the organization must see me act out the language. I must not only "talk the talk, but walk the walk." My success at this can be measured by asking, "Whom have I served today?"

One Saturday afternoon, when our maintenance company came into one of our service departments to clean, I was there waiting for them in my work clothes. Obviously, they were surprised. I told them that I was disappointed about the cleanliness of our dealerships, but that it would be inappropriate for me to be critical until I demonstrated how I defined "clean." I spent the evening with them cleaning.

Developing People

As Christians, we believe that each person is created in the image of God. No matter how flawed or dull the image, each of us is the repository of value beyond description, a value so great that God sent his only Son to the cross on our behalf. Consequently, there are no "ordinary people."

This means that I must work to create a business environment that affirms the dignity and worth of each individual. At the least, this means that I cannot allow the value of a person to be equated with his or her relative position within the organization. Every person has a right to be affirmed as having value that extends beyond his or her ability to produce work. Respect and dignity flow from the fact that we are created in the image of God, not that we are able to produce at a certain level.

A consequence of being made in the image of God is that we are co-creators with God in this world. We seek to bring expression to this belief. The desire to understand, to learn, to grow, and to develop are intrinsic to the very foundation of our being.

As a leader committed to exercising my authority through service, I have attempted to develop a corporate paradigm for the development of people. I have written a lengthy essay on this topic. Based on biblical values, the piece is distributed throughout the company. Now we are developing a number of seminars with learning exercises that address these key values.

"Second Chances" is the theme of our program for personal development, and that is the primary value in the paradigm. We have defined second chances as the space or freedom for failure as we strive to improve. We recognize that we will make mistakes, but we believe that this program points to the profound concept of grace. It provides the opportunity for a second chance for those who are trying to grow and improve. Without grace, there is no hope for genuine personal growth. Building on this is the concept of reflective openness—a willingness to challenge our own ideas, to look truthfully at who we are and what we do. Reflective openness is grounded in an approach to life that is marked by openness to change and a willingness to learn. Central is the belief that every person has equal value and is capable of teaching us something new. It implies a deep humility before the truth that none of us has all the answers.

The apex of our paradigm for the development of people is personal development, the molding of individual competency and character. This concept implies a great deal more than simply being good at one's job. Personal competency means living an integrated life. For those in leadership, it means that we must recognize the interconnectedness of life.

Each sphere of life—family, work, friends, civic, recreation—has an impact on the others. Leaders who are committed to the development of their people care about the whole person, and they model this in their own lives.

The character of leaders is a powerful force. Leaders will get the behavior they model. When you look at the behavior of the people who work for you, you are looking into a mirror and seeing your own reflection.

Finally, the development of people means caring enough about the people in the organization not only to develop their gifts but also to hold them accountable for exercising them. If we truly believe that every person's contribution is important for the well-being of the organization, for the good of the community, then we must create a structure that promotes the growth of gifts.

Building Community

It has been said that companies are increasingly the neighborhoods of the future. Many people in our nonchurched, mobile culture will find their community life in their workplace. As relational beings created to live in community, our work life offers an opportunity for meaningful human experience.

As Christians, this provides us with an excellent opportunity to work towards creating a level of relationships that points to the kingdom of God. We believe community-building experiences must be purposefully developed. We affirm the life of the community by celebrating birthdays, sponsoring company athletic teams, sending flowers, going to company-sponsored family activities, running company blood banks, helping out in voluntary associations, cooking Christmas dinners, writing cards, holding company picnics, going to weddings, going to funerals, giving baby showers, buying graduation presents, and celebrating family days. These are all part of the community experience we try to build.

Additionally, just as we have designed a formal paradigm for the development of people, we have also created one for building community. Truth-telling is its foundation. Telling the truth means that we are relentless in our efforts to accurately describe what is really happening. We must seek to make decisions based on facts, not on opinions, rumors, or prejudices. We must have the courage to ask: What is the truth in this situation? What is the truth in this person's performance?

Truth-telling is the foundation for developing trust. Simply stated, we trust people we can believe in, and we believe in people who tell the truth. Trust develops when we know we can depend on the person beside us to do what is right. Building trust is critical for creating an environment for teamwork. When we trust each other, we can build on each other's strengths while we honestly address our individual weaknesses. We learn to see situations through the eyes of different people. As a team, the potential of our collective intelligence far surpasses what any of us can do alone. Working together, we can create a strong sense of community that is a powerful source of meaning in people's lives.

To create this sense of community, organizational structure, leadership styles, and compensation plans must be congruent with the governing commitments of the company. These elements must reinforce one another. Our organizational structure is extremely flat. We have attempted to create an environment where management's and nonmanagement's behavior is not determined by a hierarchy. Rather, it is controlled by the shared vision and values of the organization. The authority of management is not derived from its organization chart. Instead, it flows from commitment to the vision.

As you can see, we are striving to make grace and truth the two foundational values in our company. In his gospel, John wrote that when "the Word became flesh and made his dwelling among us [he was] full of grace and truth" (John 1:14). Grace and truth were the hallmarks of the incarnate Word, and I believe they are central to pointing people to the risen Lord.

In my experience this emphasis upon the relational and personal dimension of organization life creates a genuine sense of purpose and meaning in the workplace for employees. Their work begins to make a positive contribution to their lives, and they make a significant contribution to the work community.

Conclusion: Integrating Prayer

An extremely important issue for most marketplace Christians is: How can my service to Christ be infused with the power of the Holy Spirit so that my life truly reflects the kingdom of God?

The Christian tradition points to prayer as the answer to this question. But for those in the marketplace, praying about or for our work life feels awkward. For what exactly do I pray? More profit? A budget request approval? Guidance concerning difficult employees? A promotion?

The following format has been extremely helpful for me in integrating prayer into my work life. Because my personal vision and the corporate vision closely overlap, I make this a central feature of my prayer life. I pray that customers and employees might experience the aroma of Christ as we serve them, and that our service will be infused with the power of the Holy Spirit. I pray that we might have the discipline to look to others' needs before we look to our own. I pray for faithfulness to our mission as it relates to fulfilling our call to service. And I pray for forgiveness when we have failed to live faithfully to our calling.

Finally, I try to pray specifically for the organization in a structured manner. In the personal dimension, I pray for individual employees, their lives, their personal and professional struggles, and for them to come to Christ. At the relational dimension, I pray for us as a community where truth and grace might reign. I confess regularly my own shortcomings in this area. I also pray regularly for relationships, for reconciliations, and for the development of trust. Regarding the technological or systems dimension, I pray for wisdom concerning how to integrate it into the human community, how to let it assist us in fulfilling our vision of service. In the economic dimension, I pray for the profits we need to sustain our commitment to our mission, vision, and core values.

Questions for Discussion

1. How can you embody and articulate faith, hope, love, grace, and truth in your workplace so that others might taste something of the kingdom of God?

2. Seek to pray for everyone you come in contact with in the marketplace on a daily basis that your life might point to the kingdom of God. Pray for opportunities where you can concretely demonstrate the love of Jesus that transforms lives.

3. Our work itself can be a "spiritual sacrifice" where we exercise obedience to Christ. Consider offering each act you do during the day to the "glory of God." Even the most mundane work then becomes pregnant with eternal significance.

4. Reflect on the primary values you experience at work in your organization. What is the belief structure concerning the nature of reality, the source of meaning, the purpose of work, and the value of people that is providing the basis for the values that are lived out in the workplace?

CHAPTER 9

A Cooperative Founder

Craftworker as Marketplace Apostle

ALONG WITH HER COMMITMENT *to homemaking and gardening, Julia Banks was involved in the planting, nurturing, and networking of house churches in Australia and North America. She was also closely involved in founding, leading, and working in craft-shop initiatives and developed a keen interest in spirituality and journal-keeping. Julia led workshops among laypeople, seminarians, and pastors, helped produce curriculum resources, and, with her husband, co-authored a book on home churches. A few years after writing this article she developed cancer and unexpectedly died.*

At thirty-four years old, the mother of two boys in elementary school and the wife of a university lecturer, I decided to to start a bachelor of education degree but halfway through found it impacting the quality of our family life more than I wished. Over the next eighteen months, in my spare time I enjoyed the opportunity to visit elderly relatives, get to know the neighbors better, prepare lunches, help slow learners read, and attend the Parents and Citizens Association of our local school.

After eighteen months I realized that I was searching for something more but not for a return to university study. Through discussion with my husband, I became aware that what gave me most satisfaction during this time was making soft toys and puppets as presents for our nephews and nieces. The idea arose of taking a further step of finding an outlet through which I could sell them. What follows is the story of how my past experience in church-related activities had a tremendous effect on my finding a place in the world of work, and how my entrepreneurial adventure was shaped by my conviction about God's role in our activities.

The Birth of a Business Venture

A short while afterwards, though one of the little stores opposite the school came up for rent, we unfortunately did not have the capital to cover the cost. I woke up in the middle of the following night with the thought: "What if I started a craft shop and took others' crafts on consignment?" That would take care of the need for a large capital outlay. Also, "What if I involved others in the running of the shop?" That would prevent it from becoming too time-consuming. None of us would have to be at the shop every day, and we could cover for each other when children were sick and when we wanted to take holidays.

I spent the next day calling an accountant, the real estate agent, and city hall, and gradually a picture of what was involved in getting a shop started expanded. Within a couple of days, I had drawn up a prospectus and costed the operation. Was I crazy? My only retail experience, apart from that of a consumer, was six weeks behind a counter in Woolworth's when I was fifteen! I had some experience working in a bank, so I wasn't totally ignorant about handling money and accounting, but that was all.

The next question was: Where was I going to find the people to join me in the venture? The only other person I knew who had craft interests was a woman who lived several doors down the street. I felt very nervous about approaching her, particularly since I recently had said no when she suggested that I start a Bible study group for neighbors. That had not been an easy decision to make. Though part of me felt obliged to say "Yes," a larger part screamed out "No." I had done that in the past but sensed that God had something else in view. But having refused my neighbor's request, how could I now ask her to join me in something that would seem "less religious?" When the moment seemed appropriate, however, my neighbor listened patiently, asked some good questions, and showed genuine interest.

Starting a Craft Shop

The following week the two of us invited everyone we knew with an interest in crafts to a meeting at my house. There were seven at the first gathering, twelve at the next, and after that our numbers gradually grew. We felt we needed about seventy people to properly staff the venture. The group was made up mainly of housewives, college students, and retirees, few of whom had any business experience. One of these had a friend who was the member of a craft cooperative in another suburb. Through her we were able to learn about their struggles and successes, and draw on their constitution as a guide for our own.

Three months later we opened a shop, not opposite the school but in the regional shopping center. Being upstairs, on a side street, and on the edges of a main development, it was not a prime location. Although our initial membership was still only about fifty, shortly after opening our numbers swelled. That enabled us to have two people in the shop each day, with each craft person working one day per month. This kept operating costs down and meant that a bigger percentage of the sales price went to the craft producer.

We decided to give any profits left over to local charities when costs had been deducted from the income. We also agreed to have a show once a year exhibiting our best work, with the proceeds donated to charity, for example, the children's ward at the local hospital.

The cooperative's membership was divided into smaller groups according to crafts produced. The various groups represented were: potters, leather workers, spinners, weavers, embroiderers, soft-toy makers, silversmiths, jewelers, and a miscellaneous group.

Each of the craft groups was responsible for the quality and pricing of the goods they made. For example, if someone was applying to join the cooperative as a leather worker, the leather workers group decided whether there was a need for more wares in their area, whether the goods were sufficiently different from those made by other members, and whether the quality was of the required standard. Each craft group also selected a member to represent its interests at the meeting of the executive committee of the cooperative.

The executive committee was selected by vote of the membership and consisted of a president, secretary, treasurer, membership secretary, public relations officer, and the craft representatives. I was asked to be the president and remained in that position for the first three years. The executive committee met monthly, although there was a lot of business conducted by phone in the intervening weeks.

The Principles of Our Operation

The idea of managing a large group of people through small group work was not new to me. I had been introduced to it as a Girl Scout. The patrol system was used to help new recruits feel connected, to provide teams where members learned to depend on each other to serve a common goal, and to allow older members to take responsibility for teaching younger ones what they needed to know to pass their various tests.

My husband and I had used a similar model in our work as church youth group leaders, dividing the large group into smaller ones, providing them with tasks to do, and encouraging the older, more experienced members to take an active interest in younger, newer ones. In that way we hoped to train future leaders. The older members, or elders, met with us to make decisions about the life of the fellowship as a whole.

But it was through my involvement over a ten-year period with a cluster of small house churches from which I drew valuable guidance in establishing and managing the cooperative. These house churches consisted of groups of twelve to sixteen people—married couples, singles, and children. Once a week we would meet for three to four hours in a member's home for informal worship and the opportunity to learn to be a genuine Christian family. Every few weeks members of the various house churches gathered for a combined celebration, generally lasting half a day or longer.[1]

The house church model was based on a rather rudimentary understanding of what the New Testament said about the character and practices of the early church. As we sought to follow those guidelines, we found ourselves returning again and again to the Bible for new insight. The teachings of Paul came alive in a way we had never dreamed possible as we learned to appreciate the wisdom, relevance, and practicality of his advice to the infant church.

Over the years I had seen so many worthwhile endeavors (both inside and outside of the church) come to nothing because of unnecessary tensions brought on by competition, self-interest, and lack of trust. How could I translate what I had learned in these groups into principles and practices that would be acceptable to a body of people from all walks of life and with a mixture of belief systems? Realizing that it would be inappropriate to

---

1. See further Banks and Banks, *Church Comes Home*, for a detailed account of how various house churches operate.

quote the Bible, I decided to employ the language of grassroots democracy and community.

It was not hard to introduce these concepts. On the whole the members of the cooperative were people of good will. Most suggestions I made gained ready acceptance and some were improved. Once the basic ethos was set, members came forward with ideas to strengthen our direction. From the outset the whole adventure was very much a group process.

Here are some of the basic principles I was able to transfer into our cooperative business venture from my experience with the house churches.

It is important to eat and drink together. In the New Testament we are introduced to the Lord's Supper as a full meal. In Acts 2:42, in the period immediately following Pentecost, we see a picture of the early believers gathering together to "break bread," which is shorthand for saying that they shared a meal. It was belonging to a house church that helped me see the centrality of the meal. We celebrated the Lord's Supper in the context of a full meal to which everyone brought a contribution. As we ate the meal, we shared our lives. I don't fully understand why that sharing was so successful. Perhaps it was the leisurely pace of eating, which allowed time for people to interact. Perhaps the food itself provided something to talk about to ease the awkward moments, or perhaps there was something about taking food from common bowls that united us. Each meal was a sort of parable that when we came together each had something to contribute to others' well-being.

In the cooperative it wasn't possible to have a meal each time we met, but we did begin each meeting of the executive committee and of the whole body with socializing and refreshments. The small groups were encouraged to include a meal with their monthly meetings. This helped to establish a web of strong relationships that helped to defuse tensions when areas of contention arose. Group leaders also were encouraged to keep a caring eye on their members and to inform us all if anyone was sick or needed help of any kind.

Each member of the cooperative has a contribution to make. Through those passages of the Bible which speak of the church as the body of Christ (Rom 12:4–8; 1 Cor 12:12–31; Eph 4:11) I had learned that everyone had a contribution to make to our life together. While some may have more to contribute than others, none is more important than the others. I had also learned that our contributions varied in character and that this was not only good but important. The more varied the contributions, the richer our life together, and the more we were built up into the fullness of Christ. Even our weaknesses were gifts, enabling the church to grow in love, patience, faithfulness, and wisdom, stretching our imaginations and helping us not to take ourselves too seriously.

People feel free to contribute only when there is an atmosphere of love and trust. The whole person must be valued, not simply his or her gift. This made the need for "wasting" time over meals all the more important, particularly in the craft groups where people were encouraged to develop a spirit of genuine cooperation. Among other things, this meant people sharing their private craft techniques so that they could learn from each other and improve the quality of their crafts.

Significant decisions are made by the whole group. There were many occasions in house church gatherings when members suffered severe frustration at the time required to give everyone a say in the making of decisions. We were, however, committed to the principle. And not simply because we believed that it was consistent with the teaching of Paul (see Acts 16:10; 1 Cor 5:4), nor because it gave equal value to all the members. Frankly, we did it because it worked. When everyone owns a decision, it can be implemented much more quickly and without a lot of resistance and complaint. The decision may take more time to make but what follows takes much less time.

It was hard to get consensus in a group the size of the cooperative, but I was committed to getting each member to participate fully in the decision-making. All major decisions were made at meetings of the entire membership, requiring agreement by a two-thirds majority. At executive committee meetings, we would look ahead to what decisions needed to be made and examine options and consequences. Then it was the responsibilty of the craft group leaders to discuss these with their group members so that people were able to vote intelligently. The craft leaders were also asked to report any complaints that members had so that these could be addressed before they became major issues.

Look for leadership from within the group. This was perhaps the hardest principle, for no matter how hard you try, once you have used the word *leadership* those influenced by our Western culture immediately think of someone out front who is over the rest. This is not, however, the biblical understanding of leadership. Christ is the only Lord of the church. He is the head of the body and we are members of it; our task is to serve the head and each other. Nevertheless, as in the early churches (1 Cor 16:15–18; 1

Thess 5:15), it is true that within each house church there emerged what we called a pastoral center. This was made up of a small group of people who cared not just for the individuals in the group, but for the group as a whole. These people often fulfilled their roles in an inconspicuous manner. They were not necessarily the traditional leadership types; rather, they were most often characterized by faith, hope, and love.

I tried to allow this concept of leadership to inform my role as president of the cooperative. I saw my presidential role as one of enabling by encouraging a vision of what the cooperative could be. It wasn't simply my vision, though I did have a big influence on what emerged. It was more that I put forward an original vision that was flexible and encouraged others to have input so that it became a corporate vision. We all owned it.

My next task was to "pastor" those on the executive committee. I spent time with them as a group and as individuals, getting to know them, complimenting them on their work, making suggestions, and encouraging them to take initiatives and risks. I learned from them and worked to develop mutual regard and cooperation. I was very conscious of the fact that the executive committee was a model for the craft groups and so made it my prime responsibility.

Ironically, individual gifts tend to emerge when the welfare of the whole group is the preeminent concern. Today most churches teach that individuals need to look inside themselves and discover their gifts. In the house church setting we found it was when members looked outside themselves to serve others that gifts came (1 Cor 12:7). While this principle was not consciously emphasized in the craft cooperative, we learned that when members actively sought the well-being of the whole group they found themselves doing things they had never done before.

Some Consequences of the Enterprise

There were several unexpected consequences of this whole venture.

First, I came to recognize the value of my skills. For example, there were the organizational skills that I had gained in that much-despised occupation as housewife. There were also those gained in house church, namely, relational skills. But I wasn't the only one who began to recognize personal strengths and skills. All of the members of the cooperative did. As mentioned earlier, our cooperative was made up primarily of housewives, college students, and retirees. We were a very ordinary bunch of people, yet we found all sorts of abilities being drawn from us as we worked for the common good.

As time passed, it wasn't just each other's craft gifts we were enjoying, it was the fruit of each other's lives. Within a month of the shop opening, one of the members told me that she'd been able to throw away her Valium. Others spoke eloquently of the friendships they had made or the sense of purpose that they had gained. We were a happy band, a true cooperative, and our life together was marked by very little discord. It was a constant source of amazement to the members that we worked together in such harmony while other organizations were constantly in conflict.

The shop hadn't been open long before we became aware that something totally unexpected was happening. We had caught the public imagination. I began to find myself being interviewed and photographed by a number of regional newspapers. Soon after, the largest metropolitan newspaper did a two-thirds-of-a-page spread about the shop, featuring photos of me wearing products crafted by the members. Then came invitations to appear on television: one on a midday magazine-type program for women, and the other a segment of a nationally produced talk show. Next came an invitation to go on a morning radio call-in program, which lead to a seminar for the YWCA: "How to Start a Small Business."

As a result, in the weeks and months that followed, more people came into the shop not just to buy but to look around, talk with the members of the cooperative, and ask how things were going. They were pleased to see this group of very ordinary people, with no particular training in business, succeed in this adventure. There were also people who needed someone to talk to and take an interest in them. They would simply wander in off the street, casually look around the shop, maybe purchase a gift, then fall into conversation with the person behind the counter and bring out all the day's troubles. It was a very humbling experience to be trusted with peoples' cares in that way. They weren't looking for counseling: all they needed was for someone to listen.

A final spin-off from the extraordinary publicity that the shop received was that we were contacted by others with similar interests. We had the added pleasure of assisting people to set up the kind of enterprise that we had created. This happened not only in our own city but in other parts of the state. It didn't take us long to realize that we existed as much for others as we did for ourselves. This was a delightful bonus for us all. It was a special vindication for me, since I still had occasional doubts about refusing to lead the neighborhood Bible study.

Conclusion

Even after our family moved to another city, I would visit the craft cooperative to see how things were going whenever I was in the vicinity. It was pleasing to hear that its foundations had proved durable over time. Members' creations were displayed and sold at local festivals and craft shows. An annual craft exhibition was still being held where all corporate profits were given away to the local hospital and charitable institutions.

Questions for Discussion

1. Whether you are in the workforce or not, are you satisfied with the major emphasis of your life? If not, why?

2. Do you have an interest, talent, or hobby that you sense needs to be nurtured and developed in some way?

3. To what extent do you make connections between biblical principles and your actual work, not just your attitudes or relationships at work?

4. Can you see ways in which your work, work environment, and workplace structures can become more shaped by your Christian values?

CHAPTER 10

A Research Economist

Seeking the Welfare of an Island Community

DAN ETHERINGTON IS AN *agricultural economist, was senior lecturer at the University of Nairobi, and then senior research fellow in the National Centre for Development Studies in the Research School of Pacific and Asian Studies at the Australian National University. He is the visionary and founder of Kokonut Pacific Limited, which commercialized a process developed through his research. He was awarded Membership of the Order of Australia and a Sustainable World Project Medal for his contributions to sustainable agriculture and economic development in the South Pacific.*

While undertaking research as an agricultural economist at the Australian National University (ANU) in 1976, I first visited the island nation of Sri Lanka to attend an International Rubber Conference. Before the conference, I took the opportunity to visit all the perennial crop research institutes: tea, rubber, and coconut. I also visited farmers and downstream processors. The monocrop tea and rubber industries, with their single products, held few surprises, but my exposure to the coconut industry stunned me. I was fascinated, surprised, and shocked.

I was amazed by the palm itself: that it should produce regular bunches of large fruit all year round; that it had a lifespan akin to that of a healthy human. The fruit itself could be divided into a wide range of products: the husk could be made into coir fiber products, while the shell could be made into tools, ornaments, charcoal, and activated carbon. Then there was the nutritious juice followed by the flesh, which had delicious milk, cream, oil and—potentially—desiccated coconut. Then I watched with fascination as a man climbed a palm to gather the sweet nectar, or toddy, from the young flowers (inflorescence). The fronds helped support him but also were used to make thatch, mats, and baskets. A little later I took time out to relax at a beautiful resort where the décor had a coconut theme. All the structural pillars were made of polished coconut trunks. It was stunning.

It was with a glowing view of the bounteous liberality of the coconut palm that I visited a number of coconut farms. Here I was surprised to find that the farmers were relatively poor. This seemed strange given the number of different products they had to sell. I also noticed a lot of empty land under the palms.

I next visited the downstream processing. The conversion of the beautiful, clean, white flesh of a mature coconut into smoky, dirty, copra puzzled me, but I took it as a necessary evil when I visited a large copra mill and was shown the rivers of dark brown oil that flowed from the copra and into refining, bleaching, and deodorizing (RBD) processes that resulted in a lovely golden, odorless, final product. I visited sites making coconut-shell charcoal. The smoke, dirt, and evidence of child labor here and at sites making and weaving coir products out of coconut husks suggested a tropical version of the "dark and satanic mills" of the industrial revolution two centuries earlier in England.

I was deeply shocked. This experience worried my psyche. A year later, it burst out in a poem contrasting these conditions with the casino culture that was spreading so rapidly in the West. This is what I wrote:

The silent sickly dawn
Signalled the return of stinking sweat
And rust-red dust of coir husk.
Soon, too soon, cockerel calls
And the clink and clank of cattle bells
Are drowned by the all-pervading,
Slow, persisting, pounding, mind-numbing
"Thump," "thump" of diesel turning
Belts of power
And wheels of life.
Wheels turning, turning,
Sharp teeth tearing, tearing
Husk upon husk,

Transforming Daily Work into a Divine Vocation

Combing, combing
Fiber upon fiber,
Bristle upon bristle,
Dust to dust.
Noisy, clanking, banging
Wheels of life.
Hands gripping, gripping . . .
Man sweats his way to his pay
of a rupee a day.
Half an orbit away
Where night still holds her sway,
Silent smooth wheels turn
With the roll of dice
Or the click of chips for a higher price.
Croupiers call
As fortunes rise and fall.
Hearts pound in anticipation
As, with hypnotic fascination,
Wheels are turning, turning,
Wheels slowing, slowing,
Hope upon hope,
Fear upon fear,
Smoke upon smoke,
Ashes to ashes.
Wheel of fortune
Or wheel of death?
Minds grabbing, grabbing,
Stomachs sinking, sinking,
Hope slipping, slipping.
Man sweats his fortune away.
before the dawn of another day.[1]

---

1. Dan Etherington, December 27, 1978.

The year after I wrote this, I was privileged to have sabbatical leave from my university. During this time, my family and I spent three months in Sri Lanka where I focused my research on the actual and potential economics of "multi-story" cropping with particular concentration on the coconut industry. This led to the development of a computer package called MULBUD (standing for Multi-crop; Multi-time-period Budgeting) that allowed researchers and farm management advisors to work through strategies for more economic outcomes in complex "agroforestry" systems.

While the development of this package with a skilled programmer was an exciting activity, it gradually dawned on me that the major problems of the relative poverty in the coconut industry had less to do with farming systems and much more to do with the products that were being produced. My graduate students (who came primarily from the Asian tropics and the South Pacific islands) were my prime teachers, and I took the lessons learnt into a full-time research position—still at the ANU. To help ourselves make the transition, in 1986 my wife (Maureen) and I took time out to go on a retreat with the interdenominational Christian organization Youth With A Mission (YWAM), whose base was in in Hawaii.

Vocational Journey to the Islands

Prior to our departure in April 1986, Cyclone Namu tore through the Solomon Islands (SI). Namu devastated the rice fields on the plains of Guadalcanal, so much so that this industry has never recovered. Rice is now an entirely imported staple. That same month, the world price of the Solomons' major export, copra (the dried flesh of the coconut), dropped to less than half its "normal" price. Deaths in the country from malaria had increased rapidly. Population growth was much faster than the increase in national educational and medical services.

Having visited the Solomons a couple of years earlier, I really felt a burden for the country. I remember thinking that the country was "paralytic" and recalled the story of the crippled man brought to Jesus on a stretcher by four friends. Their way into the house was blocked by a crowd, but with a good dose of lateral thinking they made a hole in the roof and lowered their friend through it to Jesus. I recall praying that maybe I could be used in some way as a friend of the Solomons to bring Christ's healing to this nation—possibly through the "Tree of Life" (the coconut palm), with its wide range of potential products.

Transforming Daily Work into a Divine Vocation

On retreat in Hawaii we regularly met in small groups to pray for one another. One day it came my turn for prayer and I said that I was looking for guidance as to whether I should make the South Pacific and the coconut industry a focus for my research on my return to the ANU. Somebody said that chapter 60 in the Old Testament book of Isaiah had a relevant message. We looked at this chapter and immediately the following verses seemed to leap out at me as though highlighted.

> Who are these that float along like clouds, like doves returning to their nests? Surely the people of the islands look to me; in the lead are the trading ships, bringing your sons from afar, with their silver and gold, to the honor of the LORD your God, the Holy One of Israel, for he has endowed you with splendor. Foreigners will rebuild your walls and their leaders will serve you. (Isa 60:8–10a)

These few verses referred to so many things that were relevant to the South Pacific: islands; trading ships; migration; remittances; wealth ("subsistence affluence?"); strong faith; and the role of foreigners in rebuilding the nations. At that time, in that place, in those circumstances, I took this as very specific "guidance."

On my return to the ANU, I commenced work on two projects: the political economy of the modern Chinese tea industry and the coconut industry of the South Pacific. For the first, I worked intensively with a colleague, Keith Forster, who was fluent in Mandarin. It was an exciting project that resulted in many academic papers and a book.[2]

The second project took longer to get off the ground as I went down many dead ends trying to work out what was possible in the difficult circumstances of the South Pacific where logistics, the tyranny of distance, technology, and capital constraints were all major hurdles. All the economic advice was that the islands should stick to exporting raw copra instead of attempting to produce coconut oil locally. This was because the few existing local copra mills were running into severe management problems. An attempt to build and operate a higher-value-added desiccated coconut factory was a spectacular failure.

It took the visit to Mozambique in 1992 to break through my blinkers and push me to consider turning convention on its head. I believe that God led me in significant ways to develop what we call the Direct Micro Expelling (or DME) technology. It takes small-scale processing to the nuts rather than sending the nuts (as copra) to large factories overseas. Moving

---

2. Etherington and Foster, *Green Gold*.

from concept to initial implementation took five years. We were often discouraged but then received a boost from those we were trying to help—the farmers.

Now, with DME, a farm family can produce pure virgin oil within one hour of opening a coconut. Four or five people can produce up to sixty liters of oil per day from about 600 to 1200 coconuts (depending on the size of the nuts). We formed a company, Kokonut Pacific (KP), in 1994, to commercialize the technology. We now have DME units in all Pacific Islander countries and many in Africa, Asia, and the Caribbean. However, implementation has been very difficult. As the news bulletins record, civil strife, coups, and cyclones in Fiji, Papua New Guinea, the Solomons, and Samoa have caused them and us countless problems.

My many visits to the Solomon Islands were a mix of joy and frustration. The people were lovely to work with, and their faith, prayer life, and passion for Christ put me to shame. However, corruption, government mismanagement, wanton logging of rainforests, and the breakdown of services were very depressing. The "paralytic" was getting sicker by the day! If the cripple was a paraplegic eighteen years ago, by the time Regional Assistance Mission to the Solomon Islands (RAMSI) intervened in 2003, the country was truly quadriplegic.

Hope-Filled Hints of the Future

Our continuing links with the Solomons and the restoration of peace there encouraged me and my colleagues to "have another go." In September 2003, we started praying and planning and things began moving fast. We received a flood of phone calls, emails, faxes, and letters from the Solomons asking for our DME technology. There were conferences in Canberra where we met key Christian leaders of peace initiatives. On flights, we just happened to sit next to people with wide experience in the Solomons. Did all the unexpected inquiries and chance meetings happen just by coincidence?

For us, this all added up! We were encouraged; we were being prodded and prompted. So we booked our tickets. We flew to Honiara in February 2004. The encouragement continued on the flight when I found that I was sitting next to the governor of the SI Central Bank. He is a courageous Christian who was under enormous pressure during "the troubles" and had just been reappointed to head the bank. I had an unexpected and amazing two-hour briefing during the flight!

Transforming Daily Work into a Divine Vocation

As we moved around, there was certainly an air of hope. It was as if the nation was in the role of the prodigal son, coming to its senses and saying "I have sinned." But, although there was hope, we also sensed a mood of helplessness. While there was deep gratitude for the aid from Australia, the European Union, New Zealand, and many NGOs that were helping to rebuild schools, clinics, roads and wharfs, major concern was being expressed about how people were to pay school fees, or for medicines and fuel. As one aid official perceptively observed: "We are building pipes, but there is nothing flowing through them! Rural incomes are so depressed that folk have nothing with which to pay for the services offered by the facilities that we are rebuilding."

Our KP team thought that offering a project that could generate significant increases in rural incomes would make our visit highly relevant. We also found people desperate to find a productive use for their coconuts rather than reverting to the despised production of copra for export.

We had made prior plans to visit all the main funding agencies. However, everywhere we turned, we got the same answer: "We have no facility from which to fund income-generating projects." We had already learnt from the governor of the SI Central Bank that the Solomon Islands Development Bank was bankrupt. We found that the commercial banks will not lend outside of Honiara.

We felt we were carrying the paralytic but could find no way forward! We tried the front door, the windows, the back door—all with the same response. The problem we were faced with is one that most Solomon Islanders are faced with all the time: a nonexistent rural banking structure. Lateral thinking was required.

One day in our daily devotions we were reading the passage in the Bible in 2 Kings 4 about the widow and her little bottle of oil. What was God saying to us? What should we do? What was our "small bottle of oil?" None of us had the necessary finances, yet we seemed to be being told to "Use what you do have."

- A local Christian company had business and accounting skills and real prayer warriors. They had local knowledge, contacts, and practical experience.
- We had the technology and trainers, and we had equipment in stock. We also had access to markets.

- The Islanders had the coconuts, enthusiasm, and the people to do the work.

The solution became obvious: we were to partner with the local company. We had a mutual and profound sense that "Now is the time, do it!" They would provide the local management and we would provide the equipment and training for a project. Together we would work with local communities who had already approached us.

We moved rapidly to implement this decision. We shipped off eleven DME units, one for a training site in Honiara and ten for two other provinces. We also formed a local joint venture company: Kokonut Pacific Solomon Islands (KPSI) to oversee and train the farmers to become virgin coconut oil (VCO) producers. This required organizing the logistics of bringing the VCO to Honiara and conducting detailed quality control tests as well as implementing arrangements for internationally accepted Organic Certification protocols.

Kokonut Pacific undertook to buy all the oil of export quality. This was a calculated risk, but it was the quickest way to get cash trickling through the "pipes" to the rural areas. It was a step of faith on all our parts, but we trusted that God was guiding us.[3]

Some Principles of Prayer

We were only in the Solomons for one week but not a day passed without our being involved in prayer meetings with Islanders. We were greatly blessed and encouraged by their faith and by their love. In a small way we felt that we were "Ambassadors of Hope." Paul's encouragement of the Philippians is true:

> Don't fret or worry. Instead of worrying, pray. Let petitions and praises shape your worries into prayers, letting God know your concerns. Before you know it, a sense of God's wholeness, everything coming together for good, will come and settle you down. It is wonderful what happens when Christ displaces worry at the center of your life . . . I'd say you'll do best by filling your minds and meditating on things true, noble, reputable, authentic, compelling, gracious—the best, not the worst; the beautiful, not the ugly; things to praise, not things to curse . . . and God, who makes

---

3. A technical account of this endeavor may be found in Foale, *Coconut Odyssey*.

everything work together, will work you into his most excellent harmonies. Thanks be to God. (Phil 4:6–9 MSG)

A Postscript

Those steps of faith in 2004 have resulted in the development of a significant VCO sector of the coconut industry in the Solomon Islands. There are now seventy Direct Micro Expelling (DME) units in the country directly employing some 400 women and men in their villages, and supporting over 1,000 families that grow coconuts. About 100,000 liters of VCO are exported each year. The DME process has been introduced around the tropics, in Asia, Africa, Central America, and the Pacific. It has been an exciting journey. As a social enterprise, Kokonut Pacific has also set up the Niulife Foundation.

Questions for Discussion

1. If vocation is "a summons from God to an individual or group . . . to undertake a particular task or function in life,"[4] in this particular story of a faith journey how was the summons first delivered?

2. What key "nudges" or "signposts" can you identify in the journey, and how long did it take?

3. What preparations can we make in life so that we can be open to a summons?

4. How do you learn to see the world around you through God's eyes and match that with your training and talents?

5. How might you expect to hear God's call?

---

4. *Merriam-Webster*, s.v. "vocation (n.)," https://www.merriam-webster.com/dictionary/vocation.

CHAPTER 11

A Television Journalist

Glorifying God through Truth-Telling in the Media

Mary Munford wrote this chapter several years ago while working in Los Angeles as a television news writer. She is a graduate of UCLA, California State University Northridge, where she studied political science and journalism, and Fuller Theological Seminary, where she completed a Master of Arts in theology. She has been involved in a media group exploring the connections between faith and work and been supportive of journalists who have experienced intimidation while carrying out their work. Mary's chapter is even more relevant with the growing dominance of social media and "fake news." She has received several Emmy Award nominations for her feature reports on religion and society.

"Jean-Paul Sartre died today. And it doesn't matter." Those words tumbled out of my typewriter one warm spring afternoon in 1980, the day the great French existential philosopher breathed his last. It was a lead that never made air, and was never intended to make air, though it did give my six o'clock producer a chuckle. It served to remind us both not to take ourselves, or our work, too seriously in the stressful world of television news.

Since that day I have logged tens of thousands of hours in a TV newsroom, going about the serious work of trying to accurately relay the news of the day. And it is serious business. Despite some recent and ominous changes in broadcast news, most TV journalists, like myself, still believe we have a unique calling, a public trust if you will, to provide important and necessary information to the American people. That information helps us all to be better citizens and to lead useful, productive lives.

That conviction has been held by journalists since the very beginnings of what we now call the mass media. An early newspaper man described it well: Finley Peter Dunne said his job was to "comfort the afflicted and afflict the comfortable."[1] That sounds almost biblical. In fact, it is my personal belief that this journalistic standard is quite in line with Christian faith.

I believe in a God who commands justice and honors truth. Jesus says, "I am the way, the truth and the life" (John 14:6). As a follower of Jesus, I believe I am called both to live and to tell the truth, not just in my personal life, but in my professional life as well. I believe this is possible within a career in broadcast journalism, although it is not without its pitfalls.

The Changing Character of Television Broadcasting

An important distinction is necessary: the news organization I work for is not a ministry, not a religious group. Neither is it a nonprofit company nor a humanitarian concern. This seems obvious on the face of it, but it is still tremendously important because, while I share the same goals as the organization I work for, I do not share the same motives.

A television broadcasting concern, whether it is a network or an individual station, is first and foremost a business. Like any other business, it must make a profit if it is to survive. In this sense, ABC, NBC, and CBS are no different than General Motors, McDonald's, or Sears. But there is an added dimension. Broadcasters hold a special position within the business community because they use the public airways to distribute their programs. In a sense, broadcasters are hybrid-private, for-profit businesses that use the public airways—a limited, natural resource that belongs to the American people. Consequently, broadcasters must be licensed by the Federal Communications Commission. Every few years these licenses come up for renewal, and the owners must prove to the federal regulators that they have been operating in "the public convenience, interest or necessity."[2] To fall short of that standard means to risk the loss of their license.

Because of the licensing requirements and the lucrative nature of entertainment programs, television news historically has held a privileged position within broadcasting. Profits were made primarily through the entertainment side of the business, thus, in a sense, subsidizing newsrooms, and to a certain extent freeing journalists from the forces of the marketplace.

1. Dunne, *Dooley at His Best*, 228.
2. Head, *Broadcasting in America*, 323.

Questions of significance, headline value, and the public's need and right to know were the considerations that determined how and where and to what extent stories were covered. Journalists could afford to be altruistic; they could afford to focus on providing an important public service because the money came from elsewhere in the corporation.

But in the late 1970s, broadcast owners made an important discovery: the public wanted more news, not less. So, the owners expanded news programs on the local level to several hours every day, and the money started pouring in. Slowly new questions surfaced: How can we increase the number of our viewers and therefore pump up our profits? And how can we cut the high cost of newsgathering? These newer considerations have not yet replaced the older, traditional questions journalists ask, but a serious competition is now taking place between the two. At an increasing rate, news is beginning to be regarded as a commodity to be sold for profit, rather than as a service to be provided for the public good.

The 1980s brought a major financial setback for broadcasting. The growth of cable and home VCRs siphoned viewers away from the networks. Within fifteen years ABC, NBC, and CBS together lost nearly 30 million viewers, a third of their collective audience, and that figure has consistently gone on to diminish since. As a result, corporate profits began shrinking in geometric proportions, making it more and more difficult for entertainment programming to subsidize news.[3]

In the mid-1980s, ownership of the three big networks underwent a radical transformation. Today the three networks are owned by huge conglomerates where broadcasting is only one product among many. This fact alone has changed the corporate culture and the journalistic world for thousands of writers, reporters, producers, and news executives.

As the networks continue to lose ground to cable and home videos, and now increasingly to social media and alternative news channels, the battle for dwindling audiences rages on. No newsroom and no journalist is immune. The struggle between profit and public interest is here to stay. That is the struggle I have to live with every day.[4]

---

3. Auletta, *Three Blind Mice*, 7.

4. See further articles in Lotz, *Beyond Prime-Time*, on the change from the era of network dominance to the growth of cable television.

The Various Shades of Television News

What face does this struggle take? Take a quick look at any local television news broadcast and you will find stories that range from the trivial to the tremendously important. Middle Eastern wars, terrorism, presidential politics, the race riots, earthquakes, and unemployment. These are important subjects sandwiched in between the latest gossip involving Hollywood stars and British royalty. Not everything that comes across the airwaves is of equal value. The trouble these days, some critics charge, is that the trivial is crowding out the significant. News is becoming less information and more entertainment.

I didn't sign on for this when I first entered the news business in the early seventies. As a child of the sixties, I sat transfixed during those collective moments when television news seemed to bring us all together, whether in the excitement of witnessing a walk on the moon or in the sorrow of watching a caisson carry a fallen president. I watched television news chronicle the Vietnam War, student protests, and the fight for racial equality. And I wanted very much to be a part of that process, in fact to help write current history.

Television news still does this, and often quite well. During times of war, domestic tragedy, and national celebrations we all reach for the dial that will bring us those pictures that often remain seared into our memories. Who can ever forget, for instance, that lone, brave Chinese citizen standing for all the world to see, tiny and solitary, before an entire convoy of communist tanks near Tiananmen Square? More than a thousand newspaper words ever could, that one picture conveyed what it means to struggle to be free.

The power of pictures and the immediacy of the medium often enable television to bring to light important issues that otherwise might go unnoticed. For decades Christian relief organizations and United Nations agencies have been helping the people of Africa with famine relief. But it took a BBC documentary on Ethiopia, which eventually caught the attention of American TV, to turn hunger into an international issue so compelling that for one Saturday in 1985 the world literally rocked to the sounds of Live Aid as millions of dollars were raised to help the starving.

Television news is still able to inform and move us in a way that books, newspapers, and magazines, while good in their own way, cannot. I believe that TV news still holds an important place in American society, and I'm glad to be a part of that world.

But there is also a dark side to television. The technology that brings us pictures of inspiration—from the fall of the Berlin Wall to the courage of Magic Johnson publicly facing the specter of HIV—also brings us human depravity at unthinkable levels. More and more local news time is being filled with stories of violence, murder, the bizarre, and all that panders to our voyeuristic tendencies. While some of these stories are important enough to report, when they are played up and promoted to a ridiculous degree the entire news product is cheapened. But this kind of reporting sells. As a result, ratings go up, broadcasters can then charge advertisers more for airtime, and profits increase. Money is the driving force.

The world of television news is a murky world of conflicting values where profit and the public good are locked in an ongoing struggle. While sometimes the two values coalesce, often they are at odds. Most of the people I work with in the newsroom really do care about providing accurate and useful information to our viewers. Together we struggle to be truthful in what we do, which I believe is honoring to God.

But this is not a simple task. Sometimes we are told to write stories we would rather not, for example, stories that promote entertainment programs carried by the network. These cross-promotions are self-serving and of very little benefit to the viewer. The 1993 war of Amy Fisher is a good case in point. All three networks carried "true story," made-for-TV movies of the Long Island, New York scandal in which a young woman went to prison for shooting the wife of her alleged lover, Joey Buttafuoco. All the local news stations then carried "news stories" on their early and late broadcasts, promising their viewers that they would "meet the real people behind the story." The promoted stories carried rehashed information and gratuitous interviews that added nothing new. They were essentially manufactured stories designed to get the viewer to stay with that particular station.

Many journalists have argued against the practice, saying it hurts our credibility and cheapens our professional role as important information providers. But since cross-promotion is a way to increase viewership, and hence profits, all the networks now do it. The practice has become a part of our broadcast life. Fortunately, these types of stories do not make up the majority of news. Not yet.

Since television is a visual medium, it is very much dependent on pictures. A good picture may be worth a thousand words, but in the lingo of television news, a good picture is also worth thousands of dollars. It is a way to get viewers to stay tuned. And this, too, creates a conflict. In 1993, it got NBC into deep trouble with General Motors after the network ran a story showing a GM truck erupting in flames. The network claimed the truck was unsafe, capable of catching fire in the event of an accident; but to illustrate a fiery crash for the camera, rocket lighters were placed under the truck to make certain it would burst into flames. To settle a lawsuit, NBC admitted this piece of staging and issued a long, televised apology. Within that organization, somebody aware of the situation should have sounded the alarm before the story made air. That incident hurt the credibility of all broadcast journalists.

There are, however, many instances the public never hears about when we are able to avoid similar, though maybe not as serious, mistakes. When an editor or writer sees a staging take place, sometimes we can stop it through reasonable debate or, if necessary, heated argument before it ever makes air.

At times I have found myself in that situation. A reporter interviews a crime victim who is afraid for his safety. The reporter promises not to take his picture, but the cameraman surreptitiously takes a picture anyway. Later, the reporter changes his mind and decides to use the picture, by electronically disguising the victim's identity, even though he promised no pictures at all. A videotape editor and I catch the betrayal and convince a producer to drop the picture altogether, thus ensuring the victim's safety and our integrity. We deal with dangerous adversaries to truth on many fronts; one of them is our own desire to get and use the most compelling pictures without regard for the outcome.

The goal of any reputable news organization is to provide reliable information. While the company I work for does this well most of the time, there continues to be an erosion of journalistic values in favor of profit-making, a fact that is true for all broadcasting concerns. The company's motive, like every other company, is always profit. As mentioned earlier, often the goal and the motive work well together, but sometimes they are at odds.

The Daily Goals of a News Producer

As a journalist my goal is the same as that of my company's: to participate faithfully in the information process. But as a Christian, my motive goes far beyond that of simply collecting a paycheck. There are wider issues at stake.

Scripture teaches us that we are not our own, that we were bought with a price, therefore work cannot be just a solitary, individual endeavor to make money. God has a claim on all of my life, including the one-third I spend in the workplace. As Christians there is a collective quality to our lives that embraces even the work that we do. Certainly, I work to support myself, but as a Christian I am also called to glorify God with my life, including the hours between nine and five.

Johann Sebastian Bach, upon completion of a work of music, would often initialize each new manuscript "sdg," the Latin shorthand for *Soli Deo Gloria*, "for the glory of God." Nearly 300 years later, his efforts still provide an example for us all. Bach produced his work to make a living, but he did it ultimately for God, including the music that was not directly ecclesiastical. This, I believe, is a pattern for all Christians.

Now, I don't write sermons. In fact, the vast majority of my writing could not even be classified as inspirational, although I hope that the words I write would inspire people to listen carefully to the information being given. My topics include the consumer price index, the latest labor figures, as well as the standard news stories of violence and pain from traffic accidents and fires to yet another gang-related shooting somewhere in the social amalgam known as Los Angeles.

So how can this be to the glory of God?

First, we live in a culture that depends on information. Each morning, for instance, people want and need to know what the weather is going to be like, and in Southern California, the place where I work, they need to know about traffic congestion and major accidents so they can take alternate routes to work. It is a big-city fact of life. Television news also provides important consumer information in the areas of health, medicine, and economics. In the realm of politics, it is a working journalistic article of faith that an informed electorate is an absolute essential for a well-functioning democracy.

By writing these types of stories, my work is similar to that of any farmer, truck driver, seamstress, or shoemaker who provides necessary goods and services. This is valuable work in and of itself because it helps to sustain other peoples' lives. And it corresponds with God's own providential care for and service to the creation in all kinds of active, everyday ways. To do this well, accurately, and with integrity, is one way to glorify God on the job.

Second, this activity benefits me as well. As a journalist I use my gifts to enrich others and to help improve their lives by empowering them with information, which in turn ties me into the community of others. It keeps me from being self-focused because I do not speak into a darkened, silent sky. My words have meaning because they can be a vehicle to benefit others, even when those words do not deal directly with spiritual reality. This corresponds well with God's own communal character and activities. Doing work that places me within the larger society of God's creation is another way to glorify the God whose kingdom will one day be established on earth.

Third, in addition to "speaking the truth" by providing useful information, journalists also have the opportunity to "reveal the truth." It is their responsibility to uncover information about corruption, mismanagement, and injustice. Muckraking holds a long and honorable tradition within journalism, from the early days of newspapers to *60 Minutes*. In fact, the term *muckraking* has a distinctively Christian history, now lost to most journalists. The term entered the American vernacular in a 1906 speech by President Theodore Roosevelt when he referred to the man with a muck rake in John Bunyan's *Pilgrim's Progress*.[5]

Over and over again the Bible reveals a God who calls us both to do and to love justice. To reveal injustice, then, is yet another way of remaining faithful and bringing glory to God.

Fourth, the work of a journalist is creative. I deal with facts that need to be communicated, but there is more than one way to tell a story accurately. In television, we work not only with words, but also with pictures and sound. While I believe I am called to tell the truth, I have to get at this truth by choosing selectively; I have to decide what goes on the air and what doesn't. My raw material often consists of several pages of facts and several minutes worth of video, all of which may have to be distilled into a thirty-second news story.

This kind of work constitutes part of the creative process. And since the God we worship is the Creator, who has given us all the ability to create, this too is part of doing God's work and glorifies our Creator.

Finally, my work is contemplative. The information that I gather and must then turn around into a news story is information that comes to me from the outside world. But the process of turning that information around, the creative process of making sense out of it all, is an internal process that engages not only my mind but my heart. There is a moment right as I sit down at my computer, before any words spill forth, where I face a severe emptiness. What am I going to say? How am I going to say it? Will it be any good? That moment may last only a second or two, but it is a moment

---

5. Emery, *Press and America*, 384.

tinged with fear as well as excitement because I never know exactly what is going to come out.

When the words do flow, I experience pleasure, a little rush, perhaps even a tinge of joy. This discipline of contemplation, and the experience of joy that comes from entering into it, reminds me that I am ultimately dependent on God.

Conclusion

I am not proud of everything that goes out on our airwaves. Much of it disturbs and distresses me. But for now, I am convinced that it is better for me to stay within the system, flawed though it is, attempting to be faithful in the things I can do, staying alert to new possibilities for change, and yet recognizing that some things are quite beyond my control.

When I am present in that situation, attempting to both tell and expose the truth; when I show up every day, briefcase in hand, hopeful for the opportunity to use my creative skills to benefit others; and when I experience the deep pleasure that comes from using the gifts God has given me, then I know that what I do in the workplace is indeed an act of faith, and as such, brings glory to God.

There is a wider meaning to this work that I do because I serve a greater audience who has blessed me with a serious, though joyful, responsibility.

Jean-Paul Sartre died, and it does matter. It matters every day.

Questions for Discussion

1. How does the practice of "truth-telling" affect your own occupation? Are there ways in which your workplace engages in misinformation, deception, even lies?

2. When is it appropriate to make compromises in this area? When is it important to stand up for the truth?

3. Are there opportunities within your own occupation to help improve other people's lives, work for justice, nurture your own creativity, and attempt to live a contemplative life? As a consumer, are you frustrated with television news and entertainment programming and willing to work for change in this area? If so, write a letter to either the station's

news or program director. List the program, date, time, and channel of your concern, and briefly state it in one page.

Part 3

How Can We Be Faithful to Our Calling?

Introduction

CHALLENGES TO REALIZING OUR vocation come in many forms.

During our lives we may experience a major disruption at an individual, family, institutional, or societal level. This is what happens when there is a prolonged war that affects a large part of the population or a pandemic whose consequences last beyond any lockdown and minor infection. A friend of mine who became internationally known in his chosen field of work occasionally mused on what his life would have been like if he had been born in the previous decade. As a young adult he would have almost certainly been drafted into the armed forces and spent several years fighting opposed forces. This could have led to various possibilities—he may have been killed or so severely wounded that his choice of occupation would have been limited; his father might have lost his life in the conflict causing him to find a job after the war that would immediately bring in money to support his mother and younger siblings; his going to university and starting a job would have been delayed resulting in different opportunities and directions that he might have pursued. While none of these would have lessened his capacity for living out his life vocationally, in all likelihood it would have partly or even significantly altered the form it took.

Another example is the coronavirus pandemic that substantially affected the working conditions of a significant proportion of the population. Many were forced to change the location of their work, often to a home setting. There were some advantages to this. It reduced time spent in travel and gave them more time with other aspects of their vocational template, such as members of their family, that were under pressure. While also demonstrating that some of their work responsibilities could be undertaken outside the office, factory, or site, work-life gains were increasingly blurred by the all-pervasive presence of the phone and computer. This represents a new challenge for those seeking a balanced vocational life. Others have altogether lost their jobs. While only some of these may have already started on a vocational as opposed to merely job or career path, this could certainly slow or shift the way this is approached. In the long term, this may not make a great difference, especially as the interruption to usual patterns could bring the other benefits already mentioned. Others may find that the pandemic opens up a new or deeper perspective on understanding their vocation or even a part or full alternative to their view of it.

In what follows, I will focus on three common challenges that present themselves to any search for vocation today.

- The first is to discover what it is and then continue to discern or refine its ongoing shape and purpose.
- The second is the growing trend for work options to become either more all-consuming or more precarious.
- The third is the increasing tendency for integrity at work to come under pressure and result in unjust and destabilizing compromises.

CHAPTER 12

Discerning Personal Vocation in Everyday Settings

In most cases, those reading this book are already in a particular type of employment. This has presumably come about from a mix of factors, including personal interest, educational qualifications, and job options, as well as, perhaps, family aspirations, financial rewards, and peer ambitions. In and through these, the providence of God will have been at work and what you have read so far may have opened up further ways of detecting this or understanding the potential your work has for serving God. At various points in our life—such as ten years of experience in a job or beginning to enter mid-life—we need to check whether we should continue in our present line of work. Sometimes job retrenchments or economic changes force this upon us. Those presently joining the workforce are now told that they will probably have several changes in employment in their working life. For all these reasons, we need help in checking or discovering the link between our daily work and divine vocation.

Some Basic Guiding Principles

1. There is a connection between our general vocation as a Christian and our particular vocation.

In some Christian circles, at times there is more emphasis on Jesus as Savior than as Lord. These are two sides of the one coin and cannot be separated. We are not just called to believe in what God has done for us in Christ and seek to personally share this with others, but also to let everything we do, including our work, demonstrate to others the full range of God's activities, concerns, and purposes for our world. We must hold these two firmly together. One way we disconnect them is to declare, as some public figures declare, "my private religious convictions do not intrude on my public responsibilities." Another is to fall into the habit that the Puritan leader John Flavell warned against: "Do not be so intent upon your particular callings as to make them interfere with your general calling. Beware you do not lose your God in the crowd and hurry of earthly business."[1]

In any case, it is the kind of work we do, the way we do it, our attitude to others in it, and the influence it has, that generally open the door to others being interested in what we believe and whom we serve.

2. Vocation is more a function of serving others than developing ourselves.

We are born with certain potential abilities that can be nurtured or allowed to languish. Other abilities may be developed within us through having to deal with difficulties or opportunities life presents to us. God's Spirit enhances and directs these capacities, particularly through seeking to help others. To paraphrase Paul, if you desire to have certain gifts, focus on doing constructive things for others rather than cultivating them for yourself (1 Cor 14:2). This does not rule out seeking ways of developing our gifts, but we will achieve this best when it springs from putting others' needs, not our self-fulfillment, first.

This is where a great deal of secular thinking goes astray. For Christians, vocation is primarily about serving others, not self-actualization. To put this another way, we can best realize and fulfill ourselves through serving others. Gifts and needs are therefore inextricably connected. As the Christian novelist Frederick Buechner says, vocation occurs where "our passion and the world's needs meet."[2] For this reason, some gifts will lie latent until particular needs or opportunities arise.

3. Our vocational options are limited or at least affected by our stage in life and wider circumstances.

God does not relate to us in the abstract but in a way that takes into account our stage of faith development and actual real-life situations.

---

1. Flavell, *Mystery of Providence*, 79.
2. See "Calling" in Buechner, *Wishful Thinking*, 118–19.

Discerning Personal Vocation in Everyday Settings

The businesswoman Janet Hagberg and theologian Robert Guelich helpfully discuss the way the stage we have reached in our faith journey affects our vocational aspirations and outcomes.[3] They identify six stages in the life of faith as they influence the world of work:

Stage One: The Recognition of God

Stage Two: The Life of Discipleship

Stage Three: The Productive Life

Stage Four: The Journey Inward

Stage Five: The Journey Outward

Stage Six: The Life of Love

Although we generally move through these stages in order, these stages are fluid and cumulative, with each stage building on earlier ones. While it's possible to get stuck at any stage and stay there indefinitely, hopefully we make progress into a deeper and wiser relationship with God and understanding of life. The authors summarize the connection between each faith stage and work life.

At first, our work often feels meaningless. We think it is the issue, when actually we are the issue, not work or God. Instead of trying to run the show, we need inner transformation through living into the struggles we are having with faith, God, and life. Next, we begin trying to work out how to connect our values and work. Gradually we start to focus more on being a certain kind of person than doing a certain kind of work. Through attending more to prayer, discernment, self-care, listening, obedience, and wholeness, insight into our real work in the world begins to emerge irrespective of the actual way we earn a living. We gradually begin gravitating to the toughest, more unsolvable, issues in the world like lack of love, the need for peace, and the presence of poverty, bigotry, abuse, violence, inequality, and disease. Whether in our current work or through adjusting or changing it, we start to see our role as being a creative and helpful presence in the midst of these situations rather than always having the answers to the problems. In doing this, faithfulness becomes more important than success. After this, we become aware that our best work comes out of our weaknesses when we become more dependent on God. Through experience we learn God can do things through us we did not think possible and

---

3. Hagberg and Guelich, *Critical Journey*.

use skills we did not know we had. Finally, as our spiritual egos diminish, we move from being "servant leaders" to "leading servants," enabling us to take greater risks and experience greater creativity. We realize that the issue is less a particular than living out our calling, whatever it happens to be.

Within whatever stage we occupy in our faith journey, if some dramatic change takes place on our wider circumstances over which we have no control, God is still able to draw us towards whatever vocation he has in mind for us.

As noted earlier, a friend of mine, now a well-known biblical theologian, acknowledges that if he had been born a decade earlier, making him eligible to be drafted during the Second World War, his life might well have taken a quite different direction. He might have been seriously wounded, or worse, and therefore unable to pursue studies towards a theological degree.

By the same token, if we make choices that we feel strongly are different from God's preferences, this does not necessarily exclude us from what he has in mind. He is extremely versatile and has a wide range of strategies to bring things back on course. He also has creative alternatives for the kind of work we can do that fits his ultimate purposes. It is rarely, if ever, the case that there is only one way we can contribute to his purposes, and only one time when we could do so.

4. To fulfill our vocation, quality of character is as important as relevant skills and abilities.

This is what lies behind the advice that we should only attempt "to do what we are." It is not enough to develop certain gifts or identify relevant needs. If we do not have the right attitude and motives, others are unlikely to be receptive to what we do or we only tend to achieve short-term results. This is the point of Paul's further remarks to the Corinthians about the role of love and associated virtues in our efforts (1 Cor 13:1–4). Without these, much of what we attempt will be in vain.

A story may help here. Many years ago, I was talking with a student friend in his final year of theological study. Two congregations had invited him to join their staffs and he was trying to work out which one he should accept. I asked him various questions about these two places and what they wanted him to do. The more we talked, the more I sensed that he was approaching the issue from the wrong angle. God was more interested in who he wanted my younger friend to become, rather than what he wanted him to do. As this was possible if he accepted either of the two invitations, God did not mind which invitation he accepted. My student friend was free to choose whichever he wished.

5. *While some elements of our vocation may not change, most likely the ways we fulfill it will.*

God does not provide set blueprints for what he wants us to do. There may be some consistent threads in our vocation at work, but the forms they take will vary according to external factors over which we have no control as well as the season of life we are in. The balance or mix of its other elements—family, church, civic, and leisure components—will vary at different times in our lives.

As noted earlier, Generation Y is less likely than previous generations to put all their vocational eggs in one basket. Though this could have limitations, in other respects it opens up more opportunities to consider God's call. Those who have a less flexible approach to work and life might also come up against limitations and need to put more effort into voluntary work in the community or satisfying hobbies around the house. Where both partners in a marriage are employed, if one partner's work has had priority over a period of time, he or she may need to adjust present arrangements so their spouse can do this.

The importance of having a sense of vocation in one's work was underlined in a survey organized by the Christian business author and consultant William Diehl.[4] In its opening pages he talks about how he had been twenty years in the workforce before he heard a sermon fully devoted to work. He concluded from this that work must not matter much to God. Through his denominational connections, he decided to survey 200 Lutheran CEOs to find out how they viewed the connection between their work and their service of God. When asked whether they had experienced a call from God, those surveyed uniformly said no. For them, a call was something that only happened to ministers or missionaries. Yet when he went on to ask whether they felt they were in the place God wanted them to be, and doing the work God wanted them to do, 30 percent said yes. After comparing their responses with the remaining 70 percent of the sample, he found they did two to three times better on a wide range of issues connected to their religious commitment. Some of the areas affected were Bible reading

---

4. The surevy was shared in a public lecture by William Diehl that I organized at Fuller Seminary in 1992.

and prayer, seeking justice and building community in the workplace, and developing a modest lifestyle combined with generous giving.

Today, among people generally in the marketplace, there is a growing awareness that finding purpose and meaning in work is important.[5] This is an encouraging sign that some sense of vocation, an echo as it were of a fully Christian understanding, is reappearing in our society. However, as Gordon Preece points out, it is doing so in what is in many respects a "post-vocational" society that makes having a solid sense of purpose in work more difficult. Some have responded to this by arguing that we need a more flexible approach that sees work and vocation as flowing like a river that winds rather than flows straight and branches off in different directions that are equally worth exploring. He suggests that while earlier views were sometimes static, this approach is too fluid and therefore susceptible to personal or cultural whims. What is needed is an understanding of vocation that is "rooted" in something solid but which has "wings," enabling it to pursue new or alternative ways of fulfilling that.

Steps to Evaluating Our Vocation in the Workplace

Having identified some basic characteristics of vocation, we can turn to how we go about practically discerning this. While there is no one method or formula for this, here are some helpful pointers. These work best for those who are motivated to pursue this, have some capacity for self-understanding, can clear enough time to achieve an outcome, and are willing to experiment with possibilities. It's also important to be aware that such things as self-interest and personal reputation, family expectations and demands, financial gain and prosperity, and job security and rewards can get in the way.

Once we have got these things into perspective, we can take the following practical steps to evaluate or discover our workplace vocation.

1. Recall how our innate abilities first appeared and our first efforts to help others.

It is helpful to look for clues to these in our earlier years. Like a child's drawing, these provide a first sketch of who we are and what we do. This is often obscured by the expectations of parents, schools, and churches that make us distrust our first clumsy attempts at achieving something or assisting

5. See Beckett and MacMillan, *Purpose of Life*, 4, 7, 11.

others. The well-known author and educationalist Parker J. Palmer writes personally about this:

> A few years ago . . . a friend sent me a tattered copy of my high school newspaper from May 1957 in which I had been interviewed about what I intended to do with my life. With the certainty to be expected of a high school senior, I told the interviewer that I would become a naval aviator and then take up a career in advertising.
>
> I was indeed "wearing other people's faces," and I can tell you exactly whose they were. My father worked with a man who had once been a navy pilot. He was Irish, charismatic, romantic, full of the wild blue yonder and a fair share of the blarney, and I wanted to be like him. The father of one of my boyhood friends was in advertising, and though I did not yearn to take on his persona, which was too buttoned-down for my taste, I did yearn for the fast car and other large toys that seemed to be the accessories of his selfhood!
>
> These self-prophecies, now over forty years old, seem wildly misguided for a person who eventually became a Quaker, a pacifist, writer, and an activist. Taken literally, they illustrate how early in life we can lose track of who we are. . . . Hidden in my desire to become an "ad man" was a life-long fascination with language and its power to persuade, the same fascination that has kept me writing incessantly for decades. Hidden in my desire to become a naval aviator was something more complex: a personal engagement with the problem of violence that expressed itself at first in military fantasies and then, over a period of many years, resolved itself in the pacifism I aspire to today . . .
>
> If I go farther back, to an earlier stage of my life, the clues need less deciphering to yield insight into my birthright gifts and callings. In grade school, I became fascinated with the mysteries of flight. As many boys did in those days, I spent endless hours, after school and on weekends, designing, crafting, flying, and (usually) crashing model airplanes made of fragile balsa wood.
>
> Unlike most boys, however, I also spent long hours creating eight- and twelve-page books about aviation. I . . . had always thought that the meaning of this paperwork was obvious: fascinated with flight, I wanted to be a pilot, or at least an aeronautical engineer. But recently, when I found a couple of these literary artifacts in an old cardboard box, I suddenly saw the truth, and it was more obvious than I had imagined. I didn't want to be a pilot or an aeronautical engineer or anything else related to aviation. I wanted

Transforming Daily Work into a Divine Vocation

to be an author, to make books—a task I have been attempting from the third grade to this very moment![6]

2. *Identify what we most enjoy doing and how we are best able to serve others.*

As young adults, we sometimes get a clearer sense of these things. Initially, few of us have full choice about the work we do, even if it is in an area of interest. But if we give it our best efforts, at least we start to learn some basic vocational lessons—for example, patience, persistence, reliability, faithfulness—that will stand us in good stead for the future. We can also begin to learn which aspects of our work mean the most to us and are most appreciated. Since we are not always the best judge of these, we need to hear from others who don't just view things through rose-colored glasses. In identifying these things, we should take into account our spare-time hobbies and volunteer work as well as paid employment. Why have we chosen these particular activities? What do they tell us about our deepest interests or desires to help others? Do they confirm or complement what we mainly do or are they a more satisfying alternative to it? A good example of this happened to a member of a home group I belonged to for many years:

> Brian was married to Marilyn, and they had two small children. He worked as a television cameraman in a small city. In his spare time, he had learned the art of making guitars and become so skillful at this that a few of his friends and fellow musicians asked him to make one for them. This made him wonder whether it could become his main work. However, in the start-up period this would put the family under financial pressure and, if the venture failed, it would be difficult to find another job in television. He and his wife took their dilemma to the home group and asked them for help in deciding what to do. In the end, the couple took the risk of starting a small business, which, in time was successful. This is an interesting case of a hobby moving from a sideline to a central vocational place.

This may happen in other ways. In pursuing our vocation, we should also reflect on our dreams and even daydreams. Research shows these have a basis in real life through helping us unconsciously make sense of some of what is occurring in our lives. If we take note of them over a period of time, they can sometimes point to deeper longings within us. Since they

---

6. Palmer, *Let Your Life Speak*, 19–22.

generally do this in a coded way, they need to be interpreted. This is also the case with daydreams. Though these are sometimes escapist fantasies, sometimes they contain clues to what we would really like to happen. Keeping a diary of dreams or daydreams is one way of beginning to understand them. Another is to draw on the wisdom of someone with the ability to interpret their meaning, either from personal experience or professional training.

> 3. *Pay attention to your growing convictions, workplace processes, and unexpected experiences that may clarify your vocational direction.*

Vocational direction often occurs gradually. Much of it happens circumstantially, even though we may be aware of a supernatural hand guiding it. We should not be disappointed at this. It is the way God mostly works. Little by little, step by step, we gain a clearer understanding of what he requires of us. This results in a growing contentment and confidence in what we are doing. Though this may sometimes be challenged by doubts and disappointments, especially if we have a lower self-esteem or feel the need to constantly monitor our effectiveness, mostly we have an underlying sense that what we are doing fits what God wants of us.

To some extent, undertaking job performance reviews can also be of help here. If done well, these give us a more realistic sense of what we can and cannot do. Also helpful are what are called "career construction" procedures. In these, trained counselors conduct an in-depth interview to help people identify their purpose and source of meaning in the workplace. This is designed to help us highlight:

- individual distinctiveness (skills, gifts, values), which helps determine alignment or fit with a particular work environment;
- opportunities for individuals to manage the role of work in their lives so that it contributes to their personal development;
- possibility for design, whereby the individual can approach their future career as the author of a potential future.[7]

This approach, particularly its emphasis on design, could contribute to Christians getting a clearer sense of their vocation in the workplace. Alongside this, "job crafting," a joint employer-employee project of fitting a worker's interests and skills to the actual work they do, can also come into play.

7. On some of these see Elangovan et al., "Callings and Organizational Behaviour."

Occasionally, however, we gain insight into our vocational direction in an unexpected way. Something jumps out at us or somehow seems meant for us. This does not happen very often in a workplace setting, but occasionally it does. Even then, it is generally preceded by supporting inner or external indicators. To decide whether God is really in what is happening, or whether we are just leading ourselves on, we need to draw on the normal array of checking mechanisms. Is it consonant with what God has been teaching us through Scripture? Does it persevere after prayerful consideration? Has it received encouragement from others close to us? Would it survive an initial "road test" to see what happens? No matter how extraordinary, any experience of this kind should be thoroughly cross-examined from all these angles.

4. *At pivotal moments in our lives, it might be helpful to seek help from a special discernment group.*

This practice has its roots in long-established Quaker tradition.[8] A group made up of people from different aspects of your life is called together for an afternoon or evening. For it to work, there needs to be a strong element of trust, a capacity for listening, respect for Scripture, and a humble attitude.

A typical meeting goes something like this. It begins with a period of silence so everyone can focus on its purpose, after which the person who has called it gives a brief summary of their work situation. Over the next hour or so, other members can ask questions to gain further clarity of the situation, not to give advice, share their experience, or satisfy their curiosity. The group's task is not to make the decision for the person asking for assistance but to help them approach it as objectively yet as openly as possible.

The group can pursue this in other ways. This might be through a time for reflection by any member of the group on what has been said so far; a time of affirming the most appreciated gifts of the person who has called it; a time when that person may ask the group questions that could aid their decision. After this, it is helpful to include an opportunity for prayer through which an additional insight or relevant Scripture may emerge. At the end of the session, the convenor of the group may share any wisdom they have gained regarding their situation. I have initiated such a group at two points in my life and both times found it immensely helpful.

---

8. The following draws from Farnham et al., *Listening Hearts*, 29–35.

Ways in which our wider church community can help include the following:

- raising the importance of work and vocation regularly in sermons, studies, and small groups;
- assisting members, even from a young age, to discover and exercise their God-given gifts;
- holding occasional "vocational days" in which older members share how they discerned their particular line of work;
- providing opportunities for members to give an account of their ministry in the workplace;
- helping those who are between jobs or unemployed to find, value, and fulfill activities of a vocational kind;
- developing groups made up purely of workers to share and discuss their experiences at work from a Christian perspective;
- encouraging people to fashion a spirituality that is specifically relevant to their work and workplaces.[9]

5. *We learn as much through hardships, disappointments, perplexity, and failures as through everything going well.*

As Parker Palmer comments:

> The journey bears no resemblance to the trouble-free "travel packages" sold by the tourism industry but is more akin to going on a "pilgrimage." A key part of the story is recognizing the shadow parts of our lives as well as times when God feels distant, and our work seems to make little difference, producing little from our work.[10]

We should not hide this since, as Palmer adds, "many young people today journey in the dark, as the young always have, and we elders do them a disservice when we withhold the shadowy parts of our lives. When I was young . . . most of them pretended that success was all they had ever known."[5]

---

9. See further Diehl, *Ministry in Daily Life*.
10. Palmer, *Let Your Life Speak*, 17–18.

If we fail to own this part of our lives, we aim at being too like someone else, such as a role model we admire, or trying to do something beyond our reach, good in itself but not part of God's purpose for us.

CHAPTER 13

Increasing Job Turnover and the Casualizing of Work

IN MY OWN CULTURE, during the last five years half of all workers have changed jobs, indicating how far the workplace has changed from the time of the "organization man" of the 1950s,[1] who could look forward to a lifetime career in a single firm. Significant mobility of workers now occurs at all levels and in most fields of employment.

The phenomenon of casual work has also been with us for a long time. Mostly it was confined to limited kinds of work and groups of people. It affected women more than men, was often seasonal in nature, and only became more extensive during times of recession. Now two-thirds of all workers are concerned with the increasing casualization of work and over half expect their work to be affected by it. In our country, more than 2.5 million workers now fall into this category, and it is increasingly affecting men, full-time work, and a wider range of occupations.[2] In the future we will experience greater uncertainty about where we will work, the kind of work we will do, and the amount of regular work that will be available. While this unpredictability may be new for many of us, it is by no means new altogether. For the majority of people, having a secure job, in a specific field of work, for a stated number of hours per week, is a relatively recent phenomenon. This is still not the case for large numbers of workers in developing countries today. It is helpful to remember that some of our biblical forebears were skilled in different fields of work. Some, for example, were equally skilled as metalworkers, stonemasons, woodcarvers, and

1. Whyte, *Organization Man*.
2. See further May et al., "Rise and Rise of Casual Work."

other artistic designs (Exod 3:1–18; 2 Chr 2:7). They moved between these trades according to the projects that came their way. A few, like Paul, were bivocational, alternating between making tents and undertaking apostolic work (Acts 18:1–3; 20:33–35; Phil 4:14–16). Others, who had more difficulty in finding regular work, made themselves available for hire. In one of Jesus' parables field workers were hired at different points during the day to undertake a particular job (Matt 20:1–6; compare with Mark 1:19–20). At certain points of the year, extra people were temporarily drawn into the work of sowing (Jas 5:7, 8; Heb 4:9, 10; 2 Cor 9:6) and harvesting (Ps 126:5, Gal 3:9; 1 Cor 15:58), usually combined with religious celebrations (e.g., Exod 23:16; Deut 16:23).

These patterns have been replicated down through the centuries and still have their counterparts in developed countries today. In rural towns, many inhabitants cannot survive without cultivating abilities in several areas, drawing on them as opportunities arise. It is similar with those in poorer sections of cities who cannot find regular full-time employment. The commentator William Bridges talks about vendor workers,[3] such as telecommuters, who work for several firms at once, and work-teams that move from project to project, depending on what is available. The experience of casual work is still normal for many involved in entertainment, for example music, theater, and film. This is also the case with many shop assistants, delivery people, gardeners, painters, and employees in the hospitality industry. Seasonal work is not only undertaken by newer immigrants and backpackers but by longer-term residents who depend on it for a vital part of their annual income.

The increasing incidence of occupational change and casualizing of work should help us empathize with such people more than we tend to. We need to put ourselves more in their shoes and view day-to-day life through their eyes. The challenges that face them should gain more of our empathy and help us learn ways of confronting these challenges in practical ways.

What strategies can we call upon to cope with regular changes of jobs and employment or with the uncertainty and demands of casual work? For a few, one or another of these forms of working life is a deliberate preference and fits their vocational objectives. They prefer the variety and flexibility that they can bring. Job flexibility and casual work fits more with their personalities and ways of operating. Though these types of work produce

---

3. There is a substantial discussion of prospering in the workplace without a job in Bridges, *Jobshift*.

Increasing Job Turnover and the Casualizing of Work

particular challenges and drawbacks, there are real lifestyle advantages. If they sense that God has "designed" or "equipped" them to work in such a way, this can fit with their vocational aspiration or direction.

Most people prefer more consistent work conditions and a more direct route to achieving their objectives. Where external circumstances affect these, Christians need to find consistency and direction within. Our highly outer-directed and peer-evaluated culture makes this difficult. Acquiring more inner resilience depends on strengthening faith and hope in God.

Apart from what is needed spiritually,

- at the psychological level, such workers need encouragement to overcome feelings of inferiority they might have from no longer being in regular full-time employment;
- at the social level, they need help in finding more flexible ways of developing friendships and family relationships;
- at the physical level, at times they need financial assistance to deal with varying pay, uncertain leave arrangements, and reduced benefits;
- at the vocational level, they need help to focus less on general searches for work than on what they could contribute to specific projects or opportunities.

As around only 15 percent of organizations employing such people offer any tangible help, these need to create new provisions and procedures to improve their workers' situation. It is in their own interest to do this, as productivity, morale, and commitment are strongly influenced by such factors. As there is still little or inadequate government recognition of the increased job-shifting, part-time economy, politicians also need to lift their game in this area. While unions are more aware of the problems, they mainly seek to reverse the current trends rather than develop new rules and regulations to deal with them. In each of these areas Christians need to be more proactive, take the lead, and in some cases make it their special area of commitment until permanent change is affected.

In the meantime, it is important for churches to take up the slack and help their members deal with short-term difficulties or long-term changes. Doing this will require a significant paradigm shift in the way congregations operate. They need to take more responsibility for the everyday lives of their members rather than just their spiritual and family lives. In particular, small groups within churches must become places where people talk and pray about their work on a regular basis. They can support each other financially and materially when a member is between jobs or when work is sporadic. Christian organizations also have a role to play in developing systems, processes, and best practices for dealing with changing work patterns. In time these could provide models for their secular counterparts.

If someone finds themselves caught up in the new work economy they should seek contact with others in similar circumstances. This will help them share their common concerns, support each other, and come up with innovative ways of moving forward. One of these is resolving to include new ways of finding times of rest in their weekly irregular work patterns. These small experiences of order in otherwise unpredictable lives, become routines to which they can hold fast during the most demanding work schedules or quiet spells when they have little to do. Some of this time could be given to worthwhile hobbies, exercises, sports, projects, or causes.

Increasing Work-Based Pressure and Work-Life Imbalance

It is commonly accepted that workplace pressures and life-balance challenges have increased in the last few decades. These are present even where work prospects are stable, and on-the-job expectations are clear. Time pressures and short-term results are more evident, and boundaries between work and other aspects of life are respected more in principle than in reality. Employers define commitment as workers putting their jobs above everything else, including family. Employees seem more willing to work overtime on weekends and during holidays. Emails, iPhones, and pagers increasingly intrude on nonwork time. Legislation regulating work hours is often disregarded. Single mothers, recent immigrants, self-employed workers, and middle and senior managers feel greater pressure and work longer hours than others.

This situation is worsened by the insecurity of changing jobs and/or employers more frequently, and resorting to casual or hired work. This affects relationships with colleagues, not just financial stability and general productivity. Those in less secure forms of work are more likely to experience loneliness in the workplace. Relationships with spouses, children, and relatives, as well as relationships with friends and other believers, also tend to suffer. So does time spent engaging in pastimes, interest groups, voluntary work, and worthy causes. Those in this situation are almost three times more likely to experience stress at the prospect of losing their job or failing to find enough casual work. This makes them twice as likely to become physically ill, and five times more likely to be hospitalized.

The experience of stress is a normal part of human life.[4] Without it we would not discover our limits or achieve our objectives. It helps us to respond appropriately to the pressures of daily life, including work. It is helpful to remember that many biblical figures felt stressed at times. This is often implied in stories about them but in others it is clearly expressed. For example, Moses by all he had to do (Num 11), Jeremiah by the nature of what he was asked to do (Jer 7), and Paul by difficulties involved in what he had to do (2 Cor 11). However, the stress they experienced was not always present. At other times their work was more straightforward or interspersed with quieter periods of movement between activities.

In itself, stress is not always problematic. It only becomes so when it is disproportionate to the challenge faced or goes on for too long. When this happens, stress becomes chronic and has long-term physical and psychological consequences. According to the Social Readjustment Rating Scale, a tool frequently used in analyzing stress, changing jobs appears in the middle of the overall ranking of stress. If this becomes periodic, the level of stress will increase. Another tool, the Job Stress Survey, indicates how inadequate salary and lack of opportunity for advancement heighten the degree of stress. Casual work also creates insecurities around financial reimbursement and personal fulfillment. There is also evidence that it generates more illness, leading to increased medical expenses and less opportunity for compensation when things go wrong.

It helps us to remember that just as biblical figures experienced stress, so too this sometimes affected the balance of their lives. Paul indicates that this was an occasional difficulty he confronted (2 Cor 11:27). But there were also buffers that helped moderate its occurrence. For example:

- the provision of one day in seven free from the usual kinds of work (Exod 20:8–11),
- the restriction of work primarily to daylight hours because lighting was so poor (John 9:4),
- the interruption to regular work by celebration of the seven annual festivals (Lev 23:4–44),

---

4. On what follows, see also Banks, "Stress, Workplace."

- the value of giving time to all significant dimensions and stages of life (Eccl 3:19).

These traditions continued on into the Middle Ages when approximately one in every three days throughout the year was set aside for holy celebrations. Even after the Reformation, leading Puritans such as Richard Rogers declared that only eight hours a day should be spent working, eight hours socializing and eight hours sleeping, along with one day in seven for rest, leisure, and family. This pattern of life has been gradually subverted in our modern, work-obsessed economies and is even more disrupted by increasing job insecurity and unpredictable working hours.

Finding solutions to the consequences of work-related stress and work-life disharmony requires attention from a wide range of stakeholders. It places a heavy responsibility upon boards of directors, senior management, heads of departments, standing committees, union officials, coaches, and employers of casual as well as full-time workers. All these need to be educated in the nature, types, and effects of stress related to the workplaces for which they are accountable.[5] Materials and resources are available for this, and occasionally models of organizations that have done what is needed. In general, however, there is still a great deal to do in working out what needs to be put into practice to manage and minimize stress in their workplaces.[6]

Christians in such situations, especially those in senior positions, have an obligation to be a voice for those facing job insecurity. They need to raise the questions that others in their organizations are not asking. They should continue to insist that their colleagues confront these issues seriously. They ought to equip themselves as much as possible to help point these discussions in the most fruitful and practical directions. This is even more the case in Christian institutions where casual and volunteer work and frequent job changes often occur. Once again, these entities should work at becoming models for dealing with issues of job insecurity from which businesses in our society can learn. In encouraging this, operations like the Christian Management Association could be of significant help. Christian student and graduate groups should also be equipping existing or prospective workers for the new world of work that is emerging.

---

5. See McCallum, *Employer Controls,* for some helpful suggestions.
6. From a Christian point of view, there is Hart, *Crazy-Making Workplace.*

There is also a need for more business consultants with knowledge and expertise in this area. A few of these proceed from an overt or implicit Christian base and could reference expertise in these matters in their profile or job description. Where such people are not available, there should be a search for "elders," those with some experience of these problems in the workplace. These could at least open up discussion from personal experience and contribute whatever wisdom they have gained to those needing help.

In the meantime, small groups in the church and workplace, and believers who meet regularly over coffee or lunch, can talk informally with one another about what is happening. They can help each other identify the sources of these pressures, share how they are coping, and explore options for negotiating them. They might also consider the possibility of some kind of life-shift that sidesteps these pressures or whether there is some collective action they could help initiate.

Conclusion

Since the precariousness of work is an increasing fact of life, we should do everything we can to prepare ourselves and others, including younger generations and children, to prepare for it. As suggested, this should take place across a wide range of institutions and at all levels within organizations. This includes our churches and parachurch organizations.[7] But it also requires considerable work to take place within us. If insecurity is becoming more and more part of our daily experience, we need to ensure that our identity, purpose, and meaning lie in something deeper than work. These need to rest ever more securely in God and be supported by one another. Unless this happens, even our best efforts at dealing with our current challenges in the workplace will not achieve what is required.

---

7. On some of the wider changes that need to take place see, in the Australian context, Preece, *Changing Work Values*, 241–63; and on the global front, Thomas, *Oxford Book of Work*, 525–32.

CHAPTER 14

Maintaining Integrity and Valid Compromises

ON EVERY SIDE TODAY we hear calls for greater *integrity* in personal, professional, and public life. But few pause to reflect for long on the basic meaning of this word, the complex challenges facing anyone who seeks to act with it, and what is involved in its everyday practice. Occasionally, we meet people who give the impression that integrity is a simple matter. I once spoke with a group of Christian civil servants about the appropriateness and legitimacy of connecting private values and public policy. A leading person in the group, who had been working in the Attorney General's department for most of his life, said that in all his years of drafting legislation, he had not experienced a single moral challenge. He felt, therefore, that living with integrity was quite straightforward and did not require discussion.

On the other side are those who believe that, at least in certain occupations, integrity is impossible. In such cases, people must close their eyes to so much or make so many accommodations that they cannot maintain ethical rectitude. For some, politics is one such occupation, and the world of finances increasingly another.

A popular handbook on business ethics argues for a position between these two extremes.[1] The author rejects what he regards as the unrealistic recommendations regarding organizational integrity in most writings on the subject as well as the approach that sidelines ethical behavior. Applying Lawrence Kohlberg's stages of moral development to organizations rather than individuals, he suggests that in order to survive and compete, it is permissible in the early days of a business to operate in a less ethical way and with less concern for social responsibility. Even heroic individual efforts to

---

1. Pearson, *Integrity in Organizations,* has more on this.

act ethically are unrealistic. Over time, both individuals and organizations can raise their standard of integrity.

Unfortunately, the equation of individual and organizational moral stages of development confuses categories and is therefore inadequate. The law rightly treats organizations as adult rather than infant or adolescent corporate selves. Leaders of organizations are also adults and their behavior should be judged as such.[2]

There are, then, those who tend to be too naive, those who tend to be too skeptical, and those in between who are in danger of settling for less than we feel is appropriate to how we understand our vocation. While, as Christians, we acknowledge that our human frailty and self-centeredness sometimes draw us off course, this does not make acting with integrity impossible.

The Deeper Meaning of Integrity

What, however, do people mean when they call for integrity in the workplace? Stephen Carter, in his fine book on the subject, says that though everyone argues we need more integrity, "hardly any of us stop to explain what we mean by it." "Indeed," he adds, "the only trouble with integrity is that everybody who uses the word seems to mean something slightly different."[3]

Integrity normally refers to a trait possessed by individuals who act in a principled way in difficult situations. For example, there is the doctor who does not bow to peer pressure to conceal the full facts about a colleague's harmful negligence, the lawyer who resists the temptation to shade the truth in defending someone, or the psychologist who refuses to treat clients as cases but rather as persons. The word is also used of groups and organizations where the focus is on consistently acting in accordance with high moral standards and on their willingness to publicly defend such actions when they are questioned.

Integrity, however, means more than this, as some related terms from the same root indicate. The word *integral*, for example, speaks of what is at the core of an object or person. Having integrity is more than developing a certain skill. It refers to something more organic. Losing integrity does not just lead to having less of *something*; it means becoming less of a *someone*.

---

2. Graham, "Servant Leadership and Enterprise Strategy," esp. 151–55.
3. Carter, *Integrity*, 5–6.

"Integrity is not so much a virtue itself as a complex of virtues, the virtues working together to form a coherent character, an identifiable and trustworthy personality."[4]

As the related words *integrate* and *integration* suggest, integrity also involves consistency between the various parts of a person and his or her roles. Acting with integrity is more complex than fulfilling moral obligations. The question of how to act rightly in one's work involves more than asking, What should I do?" in a particular situation. When integrity is present, there are no discrepancies between the way a person acts in one situation versus another or in one of their roles compared with another. There is a consistency about everything a person does and a coherence in the way he or she carries out responsibilities. In a person of integrity, "there is a *togetherness* about his or her personality" that some might describe as "wholeness" and others as "holiness" of character.[5]

One indication of the renewed interest in integrity is the rise of professional ethics. Too often, however, professional ethics focuses on only moral principles without raising questions about the kind of character needed to implement them or the larger vision that motivates them. In professional ethics, decision-making is also viewed too often as an individual affair, ignoring the need to consider the influence of institutional values and culture on our actions. Ethical discussions also often take place in an allegedly value-free context in which religious or ideological frameworks are excluded. As a result, the principles expounded do not have a ground of support that justifies their selection over that of others.

Since an increasing number of occupations, including many trades, now consider themselves to involve professional work, it is worth looking closer at some of the challenges that confront professionals. These are well outlined in a book written from a faith-based perspective on *Perils of Professionalism*.[6] These challenges include:

- serving the interest of an occupation rather than the people it is designed to serve and rating accountability to it higher than accountability to them,
- focusing on the ability to do one's work professionally rather than serving a demonstrable need in the community,

---

4. Solomon, *Ethics and Excellence*, 168.
5. Higginson, *Transforming Leadership*, 58 (italics original).
6. Kraybill and Good, *Perils of Professionalism*.

- protecting the secrets of professional work rather than sharing them so people can handle certain problems themselves,
- manufacturing a need that only a specialist can satisfy when there are simpler ways of dealing with it,
- overstepping one's position by performing services that exercise control rather than help the customer or client,
- using inside information gained from a client to advance one's interests in some way,
- abusing one's relationship with someone requiring help to gain sexual favors.

At the root of these practices lie three factors: the flawed personalities of the people involved, intractable values or practices in organizations, and complex situations where it is often difficult to discern what is really at stake.

What is at the heart of acting with integrity in any of these situations? One way of approaching this is to consider its presence in the lives of biblical figures. Among those who could be studied from this angle are Joseph, Moses, Rahab, Samuel, David, Nehemiah, Jonah, and Daniel.[7] Another way of addressing the issue is by asking the following questions:

- Will the action exhibit a proper regard for all the people involved, and will it exhibit a loving concern for them?
- Is it likely to lessen evil and extend justice, especially for those who are most vulnerable?
- In discussing the options, was a genuine concern for truth evident?
- Was there a recognition that a choice was involved and an avoidance of talk about "I had to do it?"
- Do both the process followed and the decision made display the virtue of patience?
- Can the decision be altered if circumstances change and another option opens up?

A contemporary approach to discussing such issues focuses on three connected perspectives, namely, an ethic of critique, of justice, and of care.

---

7. See further Higginson, *Transforming Leadership*, 54–55.

The ethic of critique considers the distribution of power and privilege and who defines what is going on in a situation. In circumstances where power and decision-making privilege are restricted to a few, it may be easier to accommodate. The ethic of justice considers who may participate, how policies are determined, whether rights are involved and for whom, and by what criteria resources are allocated. This invites a leader to consider issues of fairness and to invite participation in policy formation and resource allocation. The ethic of care concerns relationships and includes issues of dignity, human potential, and empowerment.[8]

In addition to using these perspectives, those seeking to fulfill their vocation in the workplace can make decisions and act with integrity when they approach situations in a spirit of prayer, through which God may reveal fresh possibilities; with a willingness to consult with others in a vocational or communal group; and by aiming at a win-win rather than a win-lose situation.

The Positive Role of Compromise

Though the opposite of integrity is often said to be compromise, the reality is not so simple. Compromise must not be confused with two responses that are at times intertwined with it. First, there is a difference between compromising and strategizing. The latter involves working out a long-term, often complex, set of tactics for reaching a desired end. This may involve strategic moves and countermoves, unexpected demands, and apparent concessions that are either a valid or invalid means to an end. Second, compromise is not the same as negotiation. There are appropriate and inappropriate, legitimate and illegitimate, ways of negotiating, but compromise is not necessarily involved in those that are questionable

What, then, is compromise? Mostly the word has a negative connotation. For example, it can be used to describe a decision or an action that entails a lowering of standards on the grounds of expediency or to relieve pressure. According to this, making or accepting a compromise is regarded as crossing a moral line and therefore a betrayal of one's core convictions. But the word can also be used in a positive way, as when we talk about making "a good compromise." This may involve finding a middle ground between two options based on different principles or the same principle.

---

8. See Autry, *Love and Profit*.

Maintaining Integrity and Valid Compromises

Life is full of situations in which it is not possible to do what one individually wants. Such is the case with politics, which is often described as "the art of compromise." In the world of commerce, compromise when making business deals is accepted practice. In such fields, resources, supplies, time, and personnel are often in short supply, and choices have to be made about who will receive them. People may have deeply held, conflicting opinions, and it is only through trade-offs that decisions can be reached.

A case can be made for legitimate compromise by examining the many biblical stories in which it is encouraged. A classic example is that of Naaman, the advisor to a foreign king who on a visit to Israel was healed by a leading prophet of the day. Because of the difficulty he faced as the lone believer in a foreign culture, he was permitted to bow his head in an act of pagan worship when he returned to his own country so long as he continued to give his allegiance to the true God (2 Kgs 5:15–19).

Another example is the meeting of Paul and Barnabas with the apostles and elders in Jerusalem to discuss the validity of the gentile mission. If Greek and Roman converts would agree to avoid certain actions that Jewish Christians found offensive (Acts 15:23–29), then the latter would endorse Paul's initiative without requiring Greek and Roman believers to be circumcised.

A further interesting example is Paul's apparently contradictory practice of circumcising one of his coworkers, the half-Jew Timothy, but not another, the Greek Titus. His actions reflected his stated practice of becoming "all things to all men so that by all possible means I might save some" (1 Cor 9:22). He adjusted his practice in light of people's sensitivities in order to give them unhindered access to what was most important. At the same time, he would not move an inch when he felt that doing so would jeopardize a central Christian truth. For example, he disagreed with Peter at Antioch when he encountered what he considered a betrayal of basic gospel principles (Gal 2:11–14). In all such cases, the apostle was seeking to remain true to his vocational responsibilities.

Helpful here is a recognition that many issues in life and work are not merely black or white, good or bad, right or wrong. In Proverbs and other Old Testament wisdom writings, decisions are frequently judged by whether they are wise or unwise, fitting or unfitting, appropriate or inappropriate. For example, when a person is in the presence of a superior who is at times hostile, what is appropriate is not simply a matter of their truth or falsity but whether the timing is right or the approach is sensitive (Eccl

8:2–6). There are times when it is better not to press a valid idea as it would only cause a negative response. In some cases, it is better to engage in an action that is not our first preference as it may be the best that is likely to come out of the situation.

If such a decision is the best decision in a particular situation, is it not then the will of God for us then and there, even though we may feel we should do more? For example, when Jesus was unable to heal in a certain place because the people's faith was lacking, it was not a negative compromise on his part for which he required forgiveness. If, for reasons beyond our control, we have to choose between helping one person properly and two poorly, what more can we do and what do we have to confess? If we have only a finite amount of time or number of resources, our options are limited. We may and probably should experience regret, but is more than that appropriate? Helpful here is Dietrich Bonhoeffer's distinction between ultimate (or "ideal world") and penultimate (or "real world") realities, the latter of which is constrained by actual events, situations, and people. Sometimes, as he says, the constraints we operate under require us to "sacrifice a fruitless principle to a fruitful compromise."[9] In other words, we will achieve more by maximizing what is possible, even if it is not all we would like to do, than by holding out for an ideal that is incapable of realization. Compromise is then not merely an art of achieving agreement through mutual concessions but a service to bring about the best result for the maximum number of people.

To make compromises that have integrity and achieve our vocational objectives, we should seek to have:

- a profound grasp of the way God shares his character and purposes with us since behavior basically flows from a sense of who we are and where we are heading,
- an awareness of how our life stories fit into the ongoing purposes of God and allow them to be shaped by guiding images, metaphors, and stories, as well as basic beliefs and principles in the Bible,
- a strong emphasis on the importance of character in our life journeys as integrity, including good compromises, flows more from that than from good decision-making capacities,

---

9. Bonhoeffer, *Ethics*, 67, 125–43.

- a realistic understanding of the issue at hand, with all its complexity and potential consequences, while keeping the aims and purposes of our big vocational picture in mind.

In these ways we will be able to navigate faithfully, though not always with full certainty, the challenges and opportunities that confront us in our everyday lives.

As Richard Higginson concludes:

> If compromise is to be understood in this way, it is important to affirm the element of tension. Where this lacking, compromise easily degenerates into uncritical conformity, a complacent acceptance of the "status quo." The best compromises are those which take the "promise" part of the word compromise seriously. In other words they are creative, and hold out hope of something better in the future.[10]

---

10. Higginson, *Transforming Leadership*, 58.

Epilogue

Does Our Work Have Any Eternal Value?

HERE WE ASK: Does our work have any eternal value?

Doing our work vocationally is not easy. Often it seems routine and to have little direct result. We do not always have the resources or support we need. Time feels wasted by other people's inefficiency or unnecessary red tape. Too much of our work is dominated by machines or technology. Our efforts do not always receive recognition. Workplaces are sometimes highly pressured or competitive. Our values are regarded as echoes from the past that are inapplicable to the present. Relationships with bosses or colleagues are not always cordial. We are required to work on projects that have little point. Some of our abilities lie unused and some of our ambitions unlikely to be fulfilled. At times we feel exhausted or dried up. In the midst of all this, however, we manage to do some good work and see its results. Now and again, we are able to achieve something more notable and long lasting. In such moments we get glimpses of what a better world would look like.

Fulfilling our vocation also provides inklings and pointers towards what our work contributes to God's future world. When he brings that world into being these glimpses will be transformed into a larger-than-life reality:

> As it is written, "What no eye has seen, what no ear has heard, and what no mind has conceived—the things God has prepared for those who love him." (1 Cor 2:9)

However, life in heaven will not be completely different from life in our present world. The transition from one to the other is marked by a fire that does not destroy everything from God's original creation, but refines what is unworthy and illuminates what is exemplary. We ourselves, including our bodies, will be transformed into a more glorious form of existence. Relationships with the people we have shared most closely with will also undergo change, but only for their enrichment. Whatever lies at the heart of the work we have done in a spirit of service to God, and whatever is "true, noble, right, pure, lovely, admirable, good, excellent and praiseworthy" (Phil 4:8), will be taken up by God and brought to completion and perfection.

Heaven may not, as Karl Barth hoped, contain the Louvre for all to visit, but it will contain the perfected version of the works the artists struggled to capture. The picture we are given of heaven in Revelation 21 is of:

> a city of glorious possibilities. It will be forever open (verse 25), include the best of human culture (achievements past and possibly ongoing). And although this is not in any way limited to our work, it will thus include what we have accomplished through work. For what we have done, our "splendor," will be brought and put on display as part of the "glory and honor of the nations" (verses 24–26).[1]

A captivating vision of this is contained in J. R. R. Tolkien's evocative parable "Leaf by Niggle":

> The story is about a painter named Niggle who devotes his entire life to painting a grand image that starts with a tree. The trouble is, Niggle is a perfectionist, and upon the event of his death, the only completed portion of his dream painting is one beautiful leaf. In despair at the incomplete realization of his life's work, Niggle boards the train bound for the afterlife. Imagine his joy when he arrives at the outskirts of the heavenly country and sees a tree—the very tree he had seen so many times in his imagination—"its leaves opening, its branches growing and bending in the wind that Niggle had so often felt or guessed, and yet had so often failed to catch . . ."
>
> Everyone imagines accomplishing things, and everyone finds him- or herself largely incapable of producing them. Everyone wants to be successful rather than forgotten, and everyone wants to make a difference in life. But that is beyond the control of any of us. If this life is all there is, then everything will eventually burn up in the death of the sun and no one will even be around

---

1. Cosden, *Heavenly Good*, 75.

Does Our Work Have Any Eternal Value?

to remember anything that has ever happened. Everyone will be forgotten, nothing we do will make any difference, and all good endeavors, even the best, will come to naught.

But if the God of the Bible is true, the authors say, this changes everything . . . If the God of the Bible exists, and there is a True Reality beneath and behind this one, and this life is not the only life, then every good endeavor, even the simplest ones, pursued in response to God's calling, can matter forever . . . There really is a tree. Whatever you are seeking in your work—the city of justice and peace, the world of brilliance and beauty, the story, the order, the healing—it is there. There is a God, there is a future healed world that he will bring about, and your work is showing it (in part) to others . . . Inevitably, the whole tree that you seek . . .will come to fruition. If you know all this, you won't be despondent because you can get only a leaf or two out in this life. You will work with satisfaction and joy.[2]

As Paul says to his fellow Christians at the end of his great chapter on the coming resurrection, "because of all this, be strong. Do not allow anyone to change your mind. Always do your work well for the Lord. You know that whatever you do for him will not be wasted" (1 Cor 15:58 NLT).

---

2. The fullest account of this version of Niggle's story is contained in Keller, *Every Good Endeavor,* 25–28.

Resources

ACTA audio materials by John Shea, *The Christian in the World,* 1988; John Haughey, *Towards a Theology of Work,* 1989; and Ed Marcianak, *A Worldly Vocation,* 1990.

Banks, Robert, and Linda Brooks. *Going to Work with God: Eight Bible Discussion Guides.* Sydney: Bible Society NSW, 2005.

Faith in Business Quarterly. Ridley College, Cambridge, UK. http://www.fibq.org.

Greene, M., et al. *Transforming Work: An Innovative Multimedia Group Activity.* London: London Institute for Contemporary Christianity, 2015.

Hammond, Pete, et al. *The Marketplace Annotated Bibliography: A Christian Guide to Books on Work, Business and Vocation.* Downers Grove, IL: InterVarsity, 2002.

Institute for Marketplace Transformation digital resources at *Integrating Faith and Work* http://www.imtglobal.org.

InterVarsity Christian Fellowship resources at *Ministry in Daily Life.* https://www.ivmdl.org.

Mockler Center for Faith and Ethics in the Public Square. https://www.gordonconwell.edu/center-for-faith-and-ethics/.

Stevens, R. Paul, and Robert Banks. *The Marketplace Ministry Handbook: A Manual for Work, Money and Business.* Vancouver: Regent College Press, 2005.

Theology of Work Project. https://www.theologyofwork.org.

Word in Life Study Bible. Contemporary English Version. Nashville: Nelson, 1998.

Young, Scott. "Resources for Marketplace Christians: Sampling and Evaluating the Materials." In *Faith at Work: Reflections from the Marketplace,* edited Robert J. Banks, 133–47. Eugene, OR: Wipf and Stock, 1993.

Bibliography

Agrell, Göran. *Work, Toil and Sustenance: An Examination of the View of the New Testament*. Lund, Sweden: Ohlsson, 1976.

Albrecht, Karl. *The Only Thing That Matters*. New York: Harper Collins. 1992.

Allegretti, Joseph G. *The Lawyer's Calling: Christian Faith and Legal Practice*. New York: Paulist, 1996.

Auletta, Ken. *Three Blind Mice: How the Networks Lost Their Way*. New York: Random House, 1991.

Autry, James A. *Love and Profit: Confessions of an Accidental Businessman*. San Francisco: Berrett-Kohler, 1996.

Banks, Robert. *God the Worker: Journeys into the Mind, Heart, and Imagination of God*. Valley Forge, PA: Judson, 1994.

———. "Paul as a Theological Educator: His Original Legacy and Continuing Challenge." In *Learning and Teaching Theology: Some Ways Ahead*, edited by Les Ball and Jim Harrison, 49–56. Sydney: Mosaic, 2014.

———. *Redeeming the Routines, Bringing Theology to Life*. Grand Rapids: Baker, 2001.

———. "Stress, Workplace." In *The Complete Book of Everyday Christianity*, edited by Robert Banks and R. Paul Stevens, 988–92. Singapore: Graceworks, 1997.

Banks, Robert, ed. *Faith Goes to Work: Reflections from the Marketplace*. Washington, DC: Alban Institute, 1993.

Banks, Robert, and Julia Banks. *The Church Comes Home: Building Community and Mission through Home Churches*. Salem, MA: Hendrickson, 1998.

Barth, Karl. *Church Dogmatics: The Doctrine of Creation*, Vol 3.4. 14 vols. Edinburgh: T. & T. Clark, 1961.

Beardslee, William. *Human Achievement and Divine Vocation in the Message of Paul*. Eugene, OR: Wipf and Stock, 2009.

Becket, John, and Lindsay MacMillan. *The Purpose of Life Is a Life of Purpose*. Melbourne: ReVenture, 2016.

Begbie, Richard. "The Move to the Land." MA thesis, Australian National University, 1986.

Bellah, Robert. *Habits of the Heart: Individualism and Commitment in American Society*. New York: Harper & Row, 1985.

Benne, Robert. *Ordinary Saints: Introduction to the Christian Life*. Philadelphia: Fortress, 1988.

Bernbaum, John A., and Simon M. Steer. *Why Work? Careers and Employment in Biblical Perspective*. Grand Rapids: Baker, 1986.

Bibliography

Berry, Wendell. *The Unsettling of America: Culture and Agriculture.* New York: Avon, 1978.
Bonhoeffer, Dietrich. *Ethics.* London: SCM, 1985.
Bridges, William. *Jobshift: How to Prosper in a Workplace without Jobs.* Boston: Brealey, 1995.
Brown, Colin. "Calling." In *The New International Dictionary of New Testament Theology,* edited by Moises Silva, 1:275–76. 3 vols. Grand Rapids: Zondervan, 1976.
Brunner, Emil. *The Divine Imperative: A Study in Christian Ethics.* London: Lutterworth, 1937.
Buechner, Frederick. *Wishful Thinking: A Seeker's ABC.* Rev. ed. San Francisco: HarperOne, 1993.
Calvin, John. *Institutes of the Christian Religion.* Edited by John T. McNeill. 2 vols. Philadelphia: Westminster, 1960.
Carter, Stephen I. *Integrity.* New York: Basic, 1996.
Chewning, Richard C., ed. *Biblical Principles and Business: The Foundations.* Colorado Springs, CO: NavPress, 1989.
Cosden, Darrell. *The Heavenly Good of Earthly Work.* Peabody, MA: Hendrickson, 2006.
———. *A Theology of Work: Work and the New Creation.* Carlisle: Paternoster, 2004.
Covey, Steven. *Principle-Centered Leadership.* New York: Simon & Schuster, 1992.
De Pree, Max. *Leadership Is an Art.* New York: Doubleday, 1987.
Diehl, William E. *Ministry in Daily Life: A Practical Guide for Congregations.* Washington, DC: Alban Institute, 1996.
———. *The Monday Connection: On Being an Authentic Christian in a Monday to Friday World.* San Francisco: Harper & Row, 1993.
Dunn, James D. G. *Theology of Paul the Apostle.* Edinburgh: T. & T. Clark, 1998.
Dunne, F. P. *Dooley at His Best.* New York: Scribner & Sons, 1938.
Elangovan, A., et al. "Callings and Organizational Behaviour." *Journal of Vocational Behavior* 76.3 (2010) 428–40.
Ellul, Jacques *The Ethics of Freedom.* Grand Rapids: Eerdmans, 1976.
Emery, Edwin. *The Press and America.* Englewood Cliffs, NJ: Prentice Hall, 1972.
Etherington, Dan, and Keith Foster. *Green Gold: The Political Economy of China's Post-1949 Tea Industry.* Oxford: Oxford University Press, 1993.
Faivre, Alexandre. *The Emergence of the Laity in the Early Church.* New York: Paulist, 1990.
Farnham, Susan, et al. *Listening Hearts: Discerning Call in Community.* Harrisburg, PA: Morehouse, 1991.
Fee, Gordon. *The First Epistle to the Corinthians.* Grand Rapids: Eerdmans, 1976.
Flavell, John. *The Mystery of Providence.* Edinburgh: Banner of Truth, 1963.
Foale, Mike. *The Coconut Odyssey: The Bounteous Possibilities of the Tree of Life.* Canberra: Australian Centre for International Agricultural Research, 2003.
Golsby-Smith, Tony. "The Second Road of Thought: How Design Offers Strategy a New Toolkit." *Journal of Business Strategy* 28.4 (2007) 22–29.
Goosen, Gideon. *The Theology of Work.* Sydney: Clergy Book Review, 1974.
Graham, J. W. "Servant Leadership and Enterprise Strategy." In *Insights on Leadership,* edited by Larry C. Spears, 151–55. New York: Wiley, 1998.
Greene, Mark. *Supporting Christians at Work.* London: London Institute for Contemporary Christianity, 2002.
Guinness, Os. *The Call: Finding and Fulfilling the Central Purpose of Your Life.* Dallas: Word, 1998.

Bibliography

Hagberg, Janet, and Robert Guelich. *The Critical Journey: Stages in the Life of Faith*. Dallas: Word, 1989.

Hardy, Lee. *The Fabric of this World: Inquiries into Calling, Career Choice and the Design of Human Work*. Grand Rapids: Eerdmans, 1990.

Hart, Arch. *Crazy-Making Workplace*. New York: Vine, 1993.

Haughey, John. *Converting Nine to Five: A Spirituality of Daily Work*. New York: Crossroads, 1989.

Head, S. W. *Broadcasting in America*. Boston: Houghton Mifflin, 1976.

Heintzmann, Paul. *Leisure and Rest: Biblical, Historical and Contemporary Perspectives*. Grand Rapids: Eerdmans, 2015.

Helm, Paul. *The Calling: The Gospel in the World*. Edinburgh: Banner of Truth, 1988.

Higginson, Richard. *Transforming Leadership: A Christian Approach to Management*. London: SPCK, 1996.

Hock, Ronald. *The Social Context of Paul's Ministry: Tentmaking and Apostleship*. Minneapolis: Augsburg, 1996.

Hoffman, Jan. "Clearness Committees and Their Use in Personal Discernment." 1966. https://quaker.org/legacy/atlanta/Clearness_Committees_and_Their_Use_in_Personal_Discernment.

Jericho, Greg. "We Should Be Concerned about the Casualisation of Full-Time Work." *The Guardian*, January 15, 2018. https://www.theguardian.com/business/grogonomics/2018/jan/16/we-should-be-concerned-about-the-casualisation-of-full-time-work.

John Paul II. *On Human Work* (Laborem Exercens). Boston: Pauline, 1981.

Keller, Tim. *Every Good Endeavor: Connecting Your Work to God's Work*. New York: Penguin, 2014.

Kraemer, Hendrick. *A Theology of the Laity*. London: Lutterworth, 1958.

Kraybill, Donald B., and Phyllis Pellman Good, eds. *Perils of Professionalism: Essays on Christian Faith and Professionalism*. Scottdale, PA: Herald, 1982.

LaSor, William Sanford, et al. *Old Testament Survey: The Message, Form and Background of the Old Testament*. Grand Rapids: Eerdmans, 1982.

Ledbetter, Bernice M., et al. *Reviewing Leadership: A Christian Evaluation of Current Approaches*. Grand Rapids: Baker, 2016.

Lewis, Warren H., ed. *Letters of C. S. Lewis*. London: Bles, 1966.

Lockyer, Herbert. *All the Trades and Occupations of the Bible*. Grand Rapids: Zondervan, 1988.

Lotz, Amanda, ed. *Beyond Prime-Time: Television Programming in the Post-Network Era*. New York: Routledge, 2009.

Luther, Martin. "Commentary on the Sermon on the Mount." In *Luther's Works*, edited by James Atkinson, 21:237. 55 vols. Philadelphia: Fortress, 1968.

———. "To the Christian Nobility of the German Nation Concerning the Reform of the Christian Estate." In *Selected Writings of Martin Luther 1517–1520*, translated by Theodore G. Tippert, 251–354. Minneapolis: Fortress, 2007.

———. "Treatise on Good Works." In *Selected Writings of Martin Luther, 1517–1520*, translated by Theodore G. Tippert, 97–196. Minneapolis: Fortress, 2007.

Mackenzie, Alistair, et al. *Soul Purpose: Making a Difference in Life and Work*. Christchurch: NavPress, 2004.

MacMillan, L., and J. Beckett. *The Purpose and Meaning of Work*. Melbourne: ReVenture, 2016.

Bibliography

Marshall, Paul. *A Kind of Life Imposed on Man: Vocation and Social Order from Tyndale to Locke*. Edinburgh: Banner of Truth, 1996.
Martin, Kara. *Workship 1: How to Use Your Work to Worship God*. Singapore: Graceworks, 2017.
———. *Workship 2: How to Flourish at Work*. Singapore: Graceworks, 2018.
May, Robyn, et al. "The Rise and Rise of Casual Work in Australia: Who Benefits, Who Loses?" Paper for Seminar on June 20, 2005, Sydney University.
McCallum, Ronald. *Employer Controls over Private Life*. Sydney: University of New South Wales Press, 2000.
Meilaender, Gilbert. C., ed. *Working: Its Meaning and Its Limits*. Notre Dame: University of Notre Dame Press, 2000.
"Millennials at Work: Reshaping the Workplace." *SHRM*, 2011. https://www.shrm.org/hr-today/news/hr-magazine/documents/millennials-at-work.pdf.
Miller, David W. *God at Work: The History and Promise of the Faith at Work Movement*. Oxford: Oxford University Press, 2006.
Minear, Paul S. "Work and Vocation in Scripture." In *Work and Vocation: A Christian Discussion*, edited by John Oliver Nelson, 32–81. New York: Harper, 1954.
Morgan, Tony. *The Art of Loss Adjustment*. Sydney: Morgan, 2000.
Nee, Watchman. *What Shall This Man Do?* London: Christian Literature Crusade, 1961.
Novak, Michael. *Business as a Calling: Work and the Examined Life*. New York: Free Press, 1996.
Palmer, Parker J. *The Courage to Teach: Exploring the Inner Landscape of a Teacher's Life*. San Francisco: Harper & Row, 1998.
———. *Let Your Life Speak: Listening to the Voice of Vocation*. San Francisco: Jossey-Bass, 1999.
Pearson, Gordon. *Integrity in Organizations: An Alternative Business Ethics*. New York: McGraw Hill, 1955.
Perkins, William. *A Treatise of the Vocation and Callings*. Cambridge: Cambridge University Press, 1605.
Placher, William C. *Callings: Twenty Centuries of Wisdom on Vocation*. Grand Rapids: Eerdmans, 2005.
Preece, Gordon. "Calling: Does God Call People to Work in Particular Kinds of Jobs and if so How?" *Zadok Paper*, S204, Spring 2014.
———. *Changing Work Values: An Australian Response*. Melbourne: Acorn, 1995.
———. *The Viability of the Vocation Tradition in Trinitarian, Credal and Reformed Perspective: The Threefold Call*. Lewiston, NY: Mellen, 1998.
———. "Vocation in a Post-Vocational World: The Meaning, De-Meaning and Re-Meaning of Work." In *The Bible and the Business of Life: Essays in Honour of Robert J. Banks' 65th Birthday*, edited by Simon Holt and Gordon Preece, 193–215. Adelaide: ATF, 2004.
Richardson, Alan. *The Biblical Doctrine of Work*. London: SCM, 1963.
Ryken, Leland. *The Puritans as They Really Were*. Grand Rapids: Zondervan, 1986.
———. *Redeeming the Time: A Christian Approach to Work and Leisure*. Grand Rapids: Baker, 1995.
Sayers, Dorothy. *The Mind of the Maker*. London: Methuen, 1941.
Schuurman, Douglas. *Vocation: Designing Our Callings in Life*. Grand Rapids: Eerdmans, 2001.

Bibliography

Sherman, Doug, and William Hendricks. *Your Work Matters to God.* Colorado Springs, CO: NavPress, 1987.

Solomon, Robert C. *Ethics and Excellence: Cooperation and Integrity in Business.* New York: Oxford University Press, 1992.

Stevens, R. Paul. *Doing God's Business: Meaning and Motivation in the Marketplace.* Grand Rapids: Eerdmans, 2006.

———. *The Other Six Days: Vocation, Work, and Ministry in Biblical Perspective.* Grand Rapids: Eerdmans, 1999.

———. *Playing Heaven: Rediscovering Our Purpose as Participants in God's Mission.* Vancouver: Regent College Press, 2012.

———. *Work Matters: Lessons from Scripture.* Grand Rapids: Eerdmans, 2006.

Thomas, Keith, ed. *The Oxford Book of Work.* Oxford: Oxford University Press, 1999.

Trueblood, Elton. *Your Other Vocation.* San Francisco: Harper & Row, 1952.

Tyndale, William. *Doctrinal Treatises and Introductions to the Different Portions of The Holy Scripture.* Eugene, OR: Wipf and Stock, 2007.

Veith, Gene E. *God at Work: Your Vocation in the Whole of Life.* New York: Crossway, 2011.

———. "Masks of God." *PM Notes.* https://pastormattrichard.webs.com/MaskofGod2.pdf.

———. "Vocation: The Theology of the Christian Life." *Journal of Markets and Morality* 14.1 (2011) 119–31.

Volf, Miroslav. *Work in the Spirit: Toward a Theology of Work.* Eugene, OR: Wipf and Stock, 2001.

Whyte, William H. *The Organization Man.* New York: Simon & Schuster, 2002.

Williams, David. *Paul's Metaphors: Their Context and Character.* Grand Rapids: Baker, 2003.

Wingren, Gustaf. *The Christian's Calling: Luther on Vocation.* Philadelphia: Muhlenberg, 1957.

Wolters, Al. *Creation Regained: Biblical Basics for a Reformational Worldview.* Grand Rapids: Eerdmans, 2006.

World Bank. "World Development Report 2019: The Changing Nature of Work." doi:10.1596/978-1-4648-1328-3.

Wright, N. T. *God in Public: How the Bible Speaks Truth to Power Today.* London: SPCK, 2016.

Wuellner, Wilhelm. *The Meaning of "Fishers of Men."* Philadelphia: Westminster, 1967.

www.ingramcontent.com/pod-product-compliance
Lightning Source LLC
Chambersburg PA
CBHW031500160426
43195CB00010BB/1043